No. 1
Mum

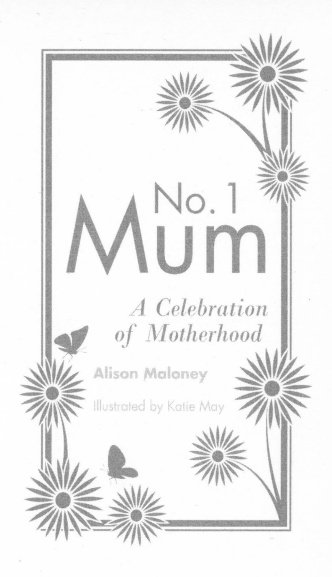

No. 1
Mum

A Celebration
of Motherhood

Alison Maloney

Illustrated by Katie May

Virgin BOOKS

2 4 6 8 10 9 7 5 3 1

First published in the UK in 2013 by Virgin Books,
an imprint of Ebury Publishing

A Random House Group Company

Text © Virgin Books 2013

Illustrations © Katie May 2013

Back cover quotation by Kate Douglas Wiggin

www.randomhouse.co.uk

Addresses for companies within The Random House Group Limited
can be found at www.randomhouse.co.uk/offices.htm

The Random House Group Limited Reg. No. 954009

A CIP catalogue record for this book is available from the
British Library

The Random House Group Limited supports The Forest Stewardship
Council® (FSC®), the leading international forest certification
organisation. Our books carrying the FSC label are printed on FSC®
certified paper. FSC is the only forest certification scheme endorsed
by the leading environmental organisations, including Greenpeace.
Our paper procurement policy can be found at
www.randomhouse.co.uk/environment

Text designed by K DESIGN, Winscombe, Somerset

Cover design by www.lucystephens.co.uk

Printed and bound in Great Britain by CPI Group (UK) Ltd,
Croydon, CR0 4YY

ISBN: 9780753541371

To buy books by your favourite authors and register for offers, visit
www.randomhouse.co.uk

Introduction

$\mathcal{F}$OR NUMBER-ONE MUMS everywhere, this is the perfect celebration of motherhood, filled with inventive ideas and clever tips and bubbling with joyful things. From chicken soup to Sunday roasts, bubble bath to balloons, *No. 1 Mum* pays tribute to the top 100 objects every mother will laughingly recognise, in an entertaining book that promises to amuse and inspire in equal measure. It's a celebration of motherhood ... in 100 objects.

After all, becoming a mum is a transformation like no other. It's a change that reaches into your heart, your soul, your home – and your handbag. (Tiny clutch bags will *never* be on the agenda again.) It's not just emotional adjustments that motherhood brings; there's a whole new array of objects to get your head around. From the wonder of wet wipes to the bottomless pit of batteries, mums soon learn the things they cannot live without! This book champions all the little things along the way that create that magic of motherhood: jolly snowmen, wet wellies, lullabies and all.

So from home-baked cookies to sky-high heels, Christmas stockings to lightbulbs (because mums are full of bright ideas...), each object in this book represents a different aspect of the superwoman that is Mum. Whether she's a domestic goddess or a professional high-flyer, she's always number one as far as her kids are concerned. Mum is one in a million. She's the person who will always put her children first and makes sure they are never left with second best. She's their number-one fan and the first in line to fight their corner.

This book is a fun-filled celebration of all the things that make this wonderful woman extra special. Because every mother ... is a *No. 1 Mum*.

Sunday Roast

NOTHING SAYS FAMILY time like the smell of a joint of meat and roasting potatoes. In the whirlwind of modern family life, the Sunday lunch or dinner is an oasis of calm, a chance for everyone to get together to catch up on their week. For Mum, once the meal is on the table, it is also a time to relax and enjoy the company of her kids without having to rush them off to dance class/football training/swimming club.

She may have to put up with the occasional moan of 'Why do we always have roast on a Sunday?' or 'Do we have to sit round the table? *The X Factor* is on', but making it a weekly ritual is an essential part of keeping the family together – and the older they get, the more they appreciate it. Many a university student or recent home-leaver has craved the comfort of a home-cooked roast and even mums love to return to the childhood home for Sunday dinner with their parents.

Most mums have the roast down to perfection, but with time-saving gravy granules so readily available, traditionally made gravy has fallen off the menu for many. It's worth resurrecting because it can really add that extra boost to the flavour. Trust Mum to go the extra mile...

Traditional Gravy

Ingredients

Juices from the meat joint

1 tbsp liquid meat fat

30g (1oz) plain flour

570ml (1 pint) stock or vegetable water

Generous slug of red wine (optional)

Method

1. Remove the cooked meat from the roasting tin and set aside to rest, covered with foil.

2. Pour the juices and the fat from the tin into a glass jug and leave for a few minutes until the fat rises to the top, then skim off the fat.

3. Place the tin on a medium hob and add the tablespoon of fat. Stir in the flour with a wooden spoon and cook for 1 minute.

4. Add the meat juices, scraping the scraps from the side of the tin, and then stir in the stock and red wine until you get a smooth gravy. Bring to the boil and allow to simmer for around 5 minutes, until the gravy is the required thickness.

To make the perfect roast potatoes, par-boil your spuds, drain, let steam dry for a couple of minutes and then return to the pan. Put the pan lid on and give them a vigorous shake to fluff up the outsides *before* putting them into the hot oil. This will make them extra crunchy and golden. But beware of over-boiling before applying this method – 8 to 10 minutes is enough – or you'll be making do with mash.

'When you're having dinner with your kids and your husband and someone says something funny or you're dying laughing because your three-year-old made a fart joke, it doesn't matter what else is going on. That's real happiness.'

GWYNETH PALTROW

Wellington Boots

THE PERFECT FOOTWEAR for family walks in the countryside, ideal for trekking through muddy forests, kicking up autumn leaves, crunching along a thick layer of winter snow, and – perhaps best of all – splashing in puddles with the little ones. These boots were *definitely* made for walking...

Medal

Because all mums deserve one.

'I want my children to have all the things I couldn't afford. Then I want to move in with them.'

PHYLLIS DILLER

Moses Basket

ONE OF THE FIRST things an expectant mum buys and one of the last things she'll want to throw out when her babies are grown. These cute little sleeping quarters are attractive, comfortable and wonderfully portable, meaning a new mum can have her tot sleeping anywhere in the house. They only get about eight weeks of use before baby's head is pressing against the wicker, but they hold a whole bunch of memories for evermore.

Handbag

WHETHER IT'S DESIGNER or high street, Mum's handbag is always massive. At the first patter of tiny feet, out go the tiny clutch-bags and purses of her youth and in comes a huge receptacle from which any number of useful things can be produced – à la Mary Poppins.

No matter how old the children get, the bag would still challenge the hand luggage policy on the average airline. It's filled with drinks, snacks, half-eaten packets of sweets, games consoles, toy cars, the whole family's mobile phones, plasters, tissues, sewing kit, hairbrush and, of course, the inevitable wet wipes.

No wonder mums enjoy escaping without the kids occasionally. A grown-up night out means taking the weight off – literally.

'A woman's mind is as complex as the contents of her handbag; even when you get to the bottom of it, there is always something at the bottom to surprise you!'

BILLY CONNOLLY

Balloons

AMONG THE MILLION roles that a mother takes on, the party entertainer is one that is called upon only on special occasions – but the merrymaking just wouldn't be the same without her. Her annual task is to make every birthday go with a bang – and we don't mean the frequent noise of popping balloons that punctuates every kid's shindig!

As well as laying on the food, this party-organiser supremo is responsible for blowing up numerous balloons, decorating the room, wrapping the prize for pass the parcel, preventing injury during pin the tail on the donkey and judging the musical statues without causing all-out mutiny. She doesn't need to wear a magician's hat or whip up some balloon animals to be the life and soul of the party. Never fazed, she has numerous party games up her sleeve, a whole stack of prizes – and the good sense to make sure that one little darling doesn't win every game and deprive the others of the coveted colouring pencils and bouncy balls...

As a change from musical bumps, try these fun party games:

BALLOON HOCKEY

This can be played outside in the garden or inside if you have a large room. You will need a packet of assorted balloons and a large cardboard box, plastic trunk or washing basket.

- Give each player a long thin balloon and a matching round or oval balloon, with each child getting a different colour.

- Turn the box or trunk on its side at one end of the 'pitch' to use as the goal.

- Assemble the children at the other end and when you say 'Go' they must attempt to push the round balloon along the floor towards the goal, using the long balloon as a stick.

- The first player to get his balloon in the box wins.

As a variation you could play with two goals, either end, and split the kids into teams, with one ball between them. The teams would then attempt to score goals while stopping their opponents from doing the same, as in proper hockey.

PASS THE BALLOON

- Inflate two different coloured oval balloons, to roughly the same size, plus a couple more reserves.

- Split the children into two teams and line them up facing the same way, as if in a queue, but a couple of steps apart.

- Give the two children at the front a balloon which they must hold under their chin. With their hands behind their backs, the players must pass the balloon back along the line using their chins.

- If any player's hands or fingers touch the balloon, or it falls on the floor, it goes back to the front of the line, and the team starts again.

- The first team to get the balloon to the back of the line wins the game.

Wrapping Paper
(and Ribbon)

*T*HERE'S SOMETHING ABOUT a gift-wrapped present from Mum that sets a high standard. Perhaps it's the care with which she creases each fold of brightly coloured paper. Maybe it's the extra flourishes: the beribboned boxes and gift tags sparkling with special flair. But above all – no matter how neat and tidy the presentation – Mum's presents to her children are always wrapped with an extra layer of love.

Birthday Cake

WHATEVER DELIGHTS MUM serves up at the annual bun-fight, the centrepiece is always the cake. It's the one thing the kids can't wait for, and will calm the over-excited party-goers down while they turn their attention to the birthday girl or boy for the candle-blowing ceremony.

Chances are Mum never baked anything more ambitious than a rock cake before the little ones came along but, being Superwoman, she will happily turn her hand to the most elaborate princess castle or pirate ship design. However, this may well result in kitchen carnage – so it pays to start simple.

Dare to Bear

This teddy bear recipe is, dare I say it, a piece of cake.

First, you need to make a basic cake mix – enough to fill two circular 22cm cake tins and three cups of a muffin tin. Preheat the oven to 170°C (325°F, gas mark 3). Grease and line the round cake tins with wax paper and place three paper cases in the muffin tin. Mix together 150g (6oz) self-raising flour,150g (6oz) caster sugar,150g (6oz) butter or margarine and 75g (3oz) unsweetened cocoa powder with three large eggs.

Fill the three muffin cases with cake mixture (no more than two-thirds full) and the remaining cups with water, then divide the remaining mixture between the two large cake tins. Bake the muffins for 20–25 minutes and the larger cake layers for 25–30 minutes. Turn out the cakes then cool on a wire rack.

Ingredients

FOR THE ICING

>100g (4oz) unsweetened cocoa powder
>2 tbsp boiling water
>350g (12oz) butter, softened
>700g (1½lb) icing sugar
>2 drops vanilla extract

FOR THE BEAR

>1 large marshmallow (halved to make two
>   circles)
>2 chocolate buttons
>1 red sweet or glacé cherry
>Red string liquorice
>A length of ribbon – for bow tie or hair ribbon,
>   depending on gender of the bear

Method

1. First, make the icing: mix the cocoa powder and boiling water together. Beat the butter and the icing sugar together until pale, then add the cocoa mixture and stir in the vanilla extract.

2. Spread a spoonful of icing directly on a cake board to 'glue' your teddy bear in place. Place one cake layer on the board, allowing room for teddy's ears. Top evenly with icing. Add second layer and cover top and sides well with icing, leaving some for decorating.

3. Remove the three cupcakes from their muffin cases. Place two of the cupcakes, wide side up, directly on the cake board (with a little icing to stick) to form the ears. Invert the last cake (small end up) onto the face to form the snout and cover all three with icing.

4. Time to make teddy's face. Place the halved marshmallows, cut side down, to form the whites of the eyes. Top with chocolate buttons, sticking with a tiny bit of icing. Then use the red sweet or cherry on top of the snout and snip the red string liquorice into small pieces to form a smiling mouth and eyelashes.

5. Form a ribbon bow and stick on to the teddy's head or neck. Ta-da!

Bubble Bath

A SMALL BUT MUCH-APPRECIATED luxury. Whatever life throws at her, a hot scented bath, filled with creamy bubbles, is the tried-and-tested way for Mum to relax after a busy day. Since Ancient Egypt, when Cleopatra demanded fresh mares' milk for her ablutions, women have known the value of a good long soak, and the joy of closing the bathroom door and sinking into a hot tub never wanes.

A plain bathwater tub is just not the same when you want to soak those aches and pains away, but don't despair if you've run out of your favourite bubble bath. Take a leaf out of Cleopatra's parchments and use the natural ingredients in your own home to create a soothing, skin-softening beauty bath.

Plain Milk Bath

Add two or three cups of fresh milk to the bath as the water is running and soak for at least twenty minutes, then use a loofah or bath mitt to get rid of dead skin. A milk bath may leave your skin feeling slightly greasy, which is no bad thing and will help in the moisturising, but you can rinse off afterwards if preferred.

Did You Know?

The Egyptian Queen Cleopatra attributed her beauty to milk – and she had a point. Lactic acid is an alpha hydroxy acid or AHA – as used in many skin creams – and is known to cleanse the skin and release dead cells. The fat in the milk also helps soften the skin, so best not to use skimmed.

Milk and Honey

Transport yourself back to the pyramids and sand dunes with another ancient beauty recipe. Put candles round the bath and imagine some scantily clad beefcakes bringing you wine and grapes as you wallow.

Pour two cups of milk or half a cup of full-fat powdered milk under warm running water and then add half a cup of honey. Swirl with your hand before taking the plunge. After your soak, brush skin with a loofah or exfoliating brush.

Scented Milk Powder Bath Salts

Ingredients

> 2 cups whole powdered milk
> ½ cup cornflour
> ¼ cup baking soda
> Essential oils for scent – e.g. lavender, vanilla or rose (see page 129 for tips on how to choose your scent)

Method

1. Put the dry ingredients into a glass jar or plastic lidded cup and shake vigorously until mixed.

2. Take off the lid and add ten drops of your chosen oil, then replace the lid and shake vigorously again. Place in a cool dark place for 24 hours to allow the mixture to cure, then use as required.

Remember milk powder does go off so continue to store in a cool place and take note of the sell-by date ... unless you want to give off the aroma of eau de sour milk!

A Glass of Wine

ANOTHER OF MOTHER'S little helpers at the end of a hectic day. A small tipple can help you unwind and a drink over dinner with your other half can add a little bit of romance to the evening meal. Moderate amounts of wine have also been seen to have a beneficial effect on health – so get those corks popping.

GRAPES OF WISDOM

A 1995 study carried out over 12 years at the Institute for Preventative Medicine at the University of Copenhagen concluded that people who drank a moderate amount of wine lived longer than non-drinkers.

- Several studies have shown that as well as benefiting the heart, wine drunk in small quantities can lower the risk of cancer.

- In 1962, an American study found that dieters lost noticeably more weight if they drank wine with their meals. Cheers!

> 'Once we hit forty, women only have about four taste buds left: one for vodka, one for wine, one for cheese, and one for chocolate.'
>
> GINA BARRECA

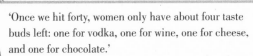

A Bottle of Wine

For the really bad days!
(But not to be advised before the kids are in bed.)

> 'Age is just a number. It's totally irrelevant unless, of course, you happen to be a bottle of wine.'
>
> JOAN COLLINS

Juggling Balls

Because if anyone can keep all the balls
in the air, it's Mum.

Baby Monitor

A BLESSING AND A curse in equal measure. The great thing about baby monitors is that you can hear every sound baby makes... The bad thing about baby monitors is that you can hear every sound baby makes!

The modern mum has come to rely on this constant connection to their sleeping baby, which these days come with all sorts of whistles and bells, including movement sensors, heart monitors and video screens so you can watch your little angel sleeping. The downside is that you may find it hard to tear yourself away ... and every breath, movement and tiny gargle is magnified into a big deal, making you jumpier than a box of frogs.

These electronic guardians have also changed the face of social situations. A friendly gathering of new parents means a row of little white boxes on the sideboard and the more anxious among them suddenly bolting from the room mid-conversation over the slightest murmurings from their precious bundle. It's much harder to ignore a crying infant when the sound is piped into the room at maximum volume.

There are other hazards involved in the use of these little wonders. Forgetting they are there while slagging off hubby/mother-in-law/dinner guest is a common experience – prompting a stony silence and extreme awkwardness when you return to the dining room.

And they have been known to pick up frequencies from nearby monitors. One lady with a video monitor had a fright when she woke up to find she was gazing at a different child entirely, and many a parent has thought there was an intruder in the house after hearing strange voices drifting over the airwaves. This can also mean you hear more of your neighbours' business than you may care to – and, don't forget, that works both ways!

Did You Know?

Chicago teacher Natalie Meilinger got a lot more than she bargained for with her video baby monitor. The tiny device picked up a signal from NASA's space shuttle *Atlantis*, giving her an exclusive view of what the astronauts were up to on their latest mission!

Wet Wipes

*T*HE PECULIAR THING about these modern-day miracles is that you don't know you need them until you are a parent. Then you find you can't live without them, even when the kids are grown up. It all begins with the baby wipes – a permanent fixture in any changing bag for obvious reasons – then it progresses to hand wipes, antibacterial wipes and surface wipes. Before you know it, you have spare packs in the car and in every room in the house. Then you squeal with delight when you discover the handy pocket packets, because you wouldn't dream of leaving the house without them.

Along with these small saviours comes a free sense of smug satisfaction. Chocolate cake smeared all over a toddler's face? Sorted. Sticky fingers from ice cream? Done. Oily hands from changing a tyre or topping up the windscreen washer? No problem.

The wet wipe is the multi-purpose must-have for every modern mum. Once used, never forgotten.

The Naughty Step

Supernanny has a lot to answer for.

'My mother had a great deal of trouble with me, but I think she enjoyed it.'

MARK TWAIN

Hand Blender
(and Ice Cube Trays)

THE HANDHELD BLENDER, stick blender or immersion blender – as it's variously called – was invented by Swiss engineer Roger Perrinjaquet in the 1950s and adopted for home use in the 1980s, becoming a hugely popular tool for mums everywhere. With a little help from baby food guru Annabel Karmel, the new gadget had health-conscious parents shunning canned baby food and literally whipping up vegetable and fruit purees to their hearts' content. Ice cube trays were then stuffed with the leftovers to freeze for another day.

All admirable stuff – until you end up with a carrot and swede puree in your gin and tonic.

Blending In

When baby purees are no longer required and the kids are happily chomping their way through house and home, there are still plenty of recipes that let your hand blender earn its keep. Here are a couple of grown-up dishes that these magical sticks can create.

RED PEPPER HUMMUS

Ingredients

      1 can chickpeas

      1 roasted red pepper, peeled and seeded

      1 tsp lemon juice

      1 tsp ground cumin

      1 tbsp extra virgin olive oil

      1 clove crushed garlic (optional)

Method

1. Drain the chickpeas and chop the pepper.

2. Place all ingredients in the plastic blender cup (or tall measuring jug) and use your hand blender to puree until smooth.

3. Chill and serve with tortilla chips, carrot sticks or pitta bread. Perfect with cocktails (see page 147) for a girls' night in!

'When you are a mother, you are never really alone in your thoughts. A mother always has to think twice, once for herself and once for her child.'

SOPHIA LOREN

Super-Simple Banana Ice Cream

This home-made dessert has only one ingredient and is amazingly easy to make. It is also so healthy it takes all the guilt out of eating ice cream on a hot day.

Ingredients

1 banana per person

Method

1. Freeze the bananas in advance, either whole or peeled and chopped.

2. Take them out of the freezer about ten minutes before you're ready to eat.

3. Peel, if using whole, and place into your immersion blender cup.

4. Blend to a smooth creamy texture and serve.

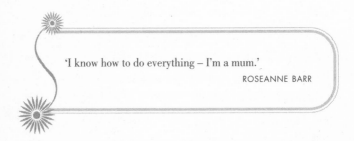

'I know how to do everything – I'm a mum.'

ROSEANNE BARR

Memory Box

THESE LOVELY KEEPSAKES are a fabulous way of storing all those little things that bring back the many stages of a child's life. It may not be an actual box – an overflowing drawer of bits and bobs or a neat folder in a filing cabinet may also fit the bill. The style of memory box will vary from parent to parent but the keepers of the special box usually fall into three categories, and their approach to this simple collection says a lot about their approach to life in general.

THE RUTHLESS RUBBISH-CHUCKER

While she no doubt adores her children, this mum is completely unsentimental when it comes to objects. If she has a memory box at all, it will be a small, uncluttered affair with some photos, a birth certificate, a favourite bedtime book (which can be passed on to the next generation in good time) and perhaps a letter or card from her child – but only if it has artistic merit!

THE SENSIBLE COLLECTOR

This lady has considered what is worthy of inclusion in her memory box and made sure it is a reasonable size for both capacity and storage. She will have an acceptable number of homemade cards from the children – but not shop-bought – plus a pair of baby shoes, one or two photos, a first tooth and a lock of hair.

THE HABITUAL HOARDER

Her treasure trove is fit to burst. She will have kept *every* card the kids gave her and piles of their artwork from school and home. Cuddly toys she can't bear to part with, even though the children have long since forgotten their existence, will make their way in there and perhaps some dolls, toy cars and favourite stories. Her keepsake collection doesn't need a shoe box – it needs a warehouse.

'You never realise how much your mother loves you till you explore the attic – and find every letter you ever sent her, every finger painting, clay pot, bead necklace, Easter chicken, cardboard Santa Claus, paper lace Mother's Day card and school report since day one.'

PAM BROWN

Making a Memory Box

Decorated or wooden boxes can be bought in shops but a personalised memory box, decorated by your children, is much more appropriate. A shoe box or a boot box should be an adequate size. Cover the box in plain coloured paper and then let the kids loose with paintbrushes, felt-tip pens and craft gems!

As you place each object in the box, write a description and any specific memories that object evokes. For example, 'Joe's first shoes, bought by Granny and Granddad in April 2005 and later worn by both his brothers. Nathan was wearing them when he took his first steps, in the back garden...' Imagine the box may be opened by someone who doesn't know all the details of the objects. Describe what is happening in treasured photos, who is in them and what date the picture was taken.

Items to include:

- A lock of baby hair

- First milk tooth to fall out

- Hospital name bracelet

- Baby hairbrush

- Booties or shoes

- First woolly hat

- Small cuddly toy

- Family photos

- Ticket to a first school play or concert

- Works of art (one or two!)

- Home-made cards (again, limited number)

- Jewellery made by the children – even if you could never bring yourself to *actually* wear it

- A favourite poem

- Notes of cute or funny things the children have said

- School report – good or bad!

- Family artefacts – such as a ring left by a grandmother or a granddad's medal

A Cuppa

WHETHER IT'S A STRONG coffee after a sleepless night or a soothing cup of tea while she listens to everyone's troubles, a cuppa plays a big part in Mum's everyday routine. That steaming mug of nectar can be the treat at the end of an arduous task, the excuse to sit down for just a minute or the necessary boost when she's been woken up every two hours by baby crying, toddler nightmares or Dad snoring!

The humble cuppa has also created social gatherings, forged friendships and brought comfort to the distressed. From coffee mornings to the casual invitation to a neighbour to 'pop round for a brew', it has been at the heart of human relations for decades: the warm hub of every home, a focal point of family life. And when the grown-up offspring pop in to see Mum, you can guarantee the first thing she'll do is put the kettle on.

Mug Shots

Fascinating facts about your daily cuppa:

- In Turkish law, a woman can divorce her husband for failing to provide her with her daily quota of coffee.

- The UK population drinks 165 million cups of tea and 70 million cups of coffee per *day*.

- More than 100 million Americans drink around 350 million cups of coffee a day.

- Scandinavia has the world's highest per capita annual coffee consumption, gulping down nearly 12kg (26.4lb) each a year.

- The cappuccino gets its name from the foamy peak on its surface, which resembles the hood worn by Roman Catholic Capuchin friars.

Tea bags were invented in the 1800s in America, to hold small samples of tea from India. Today, 96 per cent of all cups served globally are made with tea bags.

Gardening Gloves

IT'S NOT ONLY Dad who escapes to the shed for some 'me time'; mums too find precious solace among the herbaceous borders and floral delights that the garden has to offer.

Destroying a few stubborn weeds and putting your back into some digging can blast away everyday frustrations and is great exercise as well. Gardening is a fantastic stress-buster and a pleasant way to spend a sunny, warm afternoon – especially if you're the sort of mum who feels she can't bring herself to take a break without feeling guilty.

It's hard work but even the most casual gardener can reap the rewards. After all, there are few greater pleasures in life than sitting at the end of the day, drink in hand, looking at a beautiful garden that you have lovingly tended and knocked into shape ... at least until little Johnny kicks his football into your bed of prize petunias!

Gardening can also be a wonderful activity to share with the children, and a perfect way for them to learn about nature. Planting flowers and vegetables teaches them how things grow and about life cycles, and also instils patience, gardening being one of the few things in modern life that doesn't produce instant results. And in an age of pre-packed fruit and standard supermarket veg, growing edible crops goes a long way to teaching them where food comes from and the value of each morsel.

TOP FIVE

tips for gardening with kids

1. Give each child their own flowerbed or small patch of bed and encourage them to think about what they would like to plant there. If space is tight, a trough or large pot will suffice.

2. Help them choose the most practical options to avoid disappointment. Check the soil type and pH (see page 42) and decide if the patch is sunny or shady to help you select the plant varieties most likely to thrive. For younger children it is wise to do the research yourself and provide them with a small list to choose from.

3. Talk to them about what they would like to achieve – a blast of colour, a home-grown vegetable – and encourage them to think about the garden ecosystem. Perhaps you could steer them towards plants that attract butterflies and bees, such as honeysuckle, hyacinth and clematis.

4. When growing veg, choose one which everyone in the family loves to eat. It's no good growing carrots if Dad is the only one who likes them. Experiment with different varieties, such as curly kale, chard and purple sprouting broccoli.

5. Get them to prepare the soil themselves, weeding, digging it over, removing weed roots and adding compost to up the chances of success. Once the plants are in, make sure they look after the bed, watering when needed and pulling out any weeds that pop up. Explain exactly how long each plant will take to grow, bloom or fruit so that the child understands that patience is required.

'Gardens are not made by singing "Oh, how beautiful," and sitting in the shade.'

RUDYARD KIPLING

Soil Types

To make sure you're planting the right things for your garden, find out what type of soil you have. Grab a handful, run between your fingers to test the texture and make it into a ball.

It should fit in to one of the following categories.

Clay – Heavy, sticky and easily packed into a ball. Needs plenty of digging and added organic matter.

Chalky – Containing white lumps of chalk and flint, difficult to dig. Needs constant watering.

Sandy – Rough, gritty, with a sandy hue, this will not be clumped together in a ball. Has good drainage so needs lots of water in hot weather.

Silty – Usually found near rivers, this feels silky to the touch due to the small particles. It has plenty of nutrients and good drainage.

Peaty – Dark and spongy, it has a high acid content which may make some crops difficult to grow. Needs to be kept watered in the summer.

Loamy – Brown and crumbly, it is high in nutrients and drains well. Good soil for growing almost anything.

> 'Remember that children, marriages, and flower
> gardens reflect the kind of care they get.'
>
> H. JACKSON BROWN JR.

pH LEVELS

Soil-testing kits are cheap and available from any garden centre. Below are the best plants for each pH level:

Around 7: neutral – good for growing most things.

6–7: mildly acidic – root veg such as swede and carrots, pumpkins, sweetcorn, tomato.

Below 6: very acidic – fennel, sweet potato, potato, rhododendrons, camellias and heathers.

Above 7: alkaline – cabbage, cauliflower, broccoli, asparagus and leeks.

> 'If you have a garden and a library, you have
> everything you need.'
>
> MARCUS TULLIUS CICERO

Lightbulb

Because Mum is always full of bright ideas.

Tickets

WHEN IT COMES TO family days out, Mum has just the ticket – literally and figuratively. Entertaining the kids during those long summer holidays is made easier if you can plan a day out, and there are plenty of different activities to enjoy with each age group.

TOP DAYS OUT

PRE-SCHOOL AGE

Zoo or safari park – Toddlers love animals so gawping at giraffes and elephants is always a winner.

Petting farm – A great place for the children to get up close to the animals and touch them. But take antibacterial wipes and gel and make sure you follow the hand-washing rules to prevent mishaps.

Soft play centres – A reasonably cheap way to spend an afternoon. And if you go with a friend, you can have a natter over a cuppa while they have the time of their lives.

AGES 6–12

Beach – You can't beat a day at the seaside. Take a ball, a set of boules or a cricket set for added family fun. See pages 98–100 for more good games.

Theme park – Many theme parks can be a disappointment for the pre-schoolers, as height restrictions mean some rides may be out of bounds. But once they're over six, there's more chance of getting your money's worth.

Craft days – Shops and other businesses often run holiday workshops which are great for kids. They can decorate and glaze their own pottery, or try chocolate-sculpting, bear-building and loads more activities.

Bike rides – A great way to have a healthy day out and enjoy an activity together. Local council websites and cycling club sites have details of cycle routes and parks, which are safe for all.

TEENAGERS

It's not always easy to get your teenager to join in family days out – but they can be tempted with the right offers.

Cinema – A good film and maybe a pizza is the perfect day or evening out for a teenager.

Tenpin bowling – A favourite with all ages, even teens, and brilliant fun for Mum and Dad.

Ice skating – Get your skates on for thrills and spills on the ice. A day at the ice rink is filled with laughter – especially from the kids when Mum ends up on her bottom!

Portable Player

THE PORTABLE DVD PLAYER is Mum's secret weapon on long car journeys. The in-car entertainment is guaranteed to keep the kids quiet – after she's settled the initial barney about which film to watch. These natty little inventions keep the cries of 'Are we there yet?' to a bare minimum and, better still, can help with motion sickness as the kids are looking straight ahead and not staring out of the window or reading a book.

They can also be pulled out of the armoury to solve the age-old 'Whose turn to get the telly?' question. Best of all, a portable player can give Mum a bit of respite if the rest of the family is glued to a football match or *TOWIE* and she wants to sneak into a quiet corner with a good movie. Bliss!

Long journeys may require more than DVDs and good music. Here are ten ways to stave off the 'Are we there yet?' drone.

END TO END
Choose a subject – e.g. countries, animals, films, celebrities. The first player must name something in this category beginning with A. The second player takes the last letter of the previous answer as the first letter of his answer and so on. The game ends when a player repeats an answer or runs out of answers.

CAR BINGO
Before leaving the house write or draw a 'bingo card' for each player containing a list of nine items that may be spotted on your journey (woman wearing hat, 50 mph sign, police car etc). Some objects can be duplicated but each card must contain a different combination. The first person to tick off all the things on their card shouts 'House' and wins the game. You might want to play several games on a long journey, so prepare a few cards.

If you'd like pictorial sheets but haven't the time or talent to draw them, there are printable versions available on the internet.

THE MINISTER'S CAT

A great memory game which also encourages children to use imaginative adjectives. Players go through the alphabet adding a new adjective to the sentence, 'The Minister's cat is a ... cat.' Then each player repeats the sentence including all the previous answers in order (for example, 'The minister's cat is an agile, bouncy, colourful cat'), until you get to Z. If a player misses one out they are excluded.

ANIMAL, MINERAL, VEGETABLE

Player one thinks of an object or animal and all the other players take it in turn to ask him or her a question, starting with 'Is it animal, mineral or vegetable?' (i.e. an animal, object or plant). After answering this, player one can only answer 'yes' or 'no' to subsequent questions. The first player to guess what player one has in mind wins the round. It is then his turn to think of an object.

49

CONNECTIONS

This is a quick-fire game with no hesitation allowed. Player one thinks of a word – it can be an object, adjective or person – and the next says the first thing that comes into his mind, as long as it has a connection (e.g. 'hot' – 'tap' – 'dance'). The game continues round all the players until there is a repetition or hesitation.

SPELLBOUND

This is better with older children whose spelling is at a reasonable level. The object of the game is to come up with the next letter in a word *without* ever finishing it. Player one kicks off with a letter and each subsequent player adds another, having a word or words in mind should he be challenged. The player who finishes any known word, accidentally or otherwise, is out, and play resumes with the player to his left beginning a new spelling chain. For example, players one, two and three may say T, H and A respectively, then player four may say N. Although player four may have been thinking of a longer word, e.g. thank, he has completed a word and therefore is out.

CAR ALPHABET

Get the kids to spot cars whose make or model begins with each letter of the alphabet, staring with A. So it may be an Audi or a Honda Accord. Some letters are really tough

(E, Q, U are rare at the start of car names) so if one letter is taking more than five minutes, move on.

MUSIC MAESTROS
Put a familiar CD in the stereo and get everyone in the car to sing along. When they are happily singing along, turn the volume down for twenty seconds and see if they can come back in the right place when the music returns.

MOTORWAY MATCH
This can be played on any road but is a great one for motorways because of the sheer volume of vehicles. Each player chooses a car colour and make, e.g. blue Ford, silver BMW. When that player sees the colour and make of his choice he shouts 'match' and a point is awarded. This can also be adapted for animals (e.g. sheep, cow, horse) or road signs.

SWEET SILENCE
When you've finally had enough of playing games and need to give the grey matter a bit of rest, hand everyone in the car a sweet. Then see who can make it last the longest. It really does keep the kids quiet for a long while!

Car Keys

MUM'S TAXI SERVICE IS the best in town. It's free, reliable and at the kids' beck and call 24/7. It starts with the school run and after-school clubs – the judo lessons, rugby and football training, music and dance classes – then your weekends are filled with running them round to horse-riding lessons and swimming clubs, as well as umpteen birthday parties. And the older they get, the more frequent the journeys. By the time they are teenagers, you're spending your Friday nights waiting outside the school disco – not quite the sparkling start to the weekend Mum had in mind.

But it's not all bad. In a recent survey, parents complimented the 'bonding environment' of the cosy car, saying the regular journeys meant time to chat and extra time with their kids – where they could *really* communicate.

Did You Know?

If parents charged like a taxi on the meter for their chauffeur driving and waiting time, children would be faced with an annual bill of up to £10,000 a year!

Map

Because Mum is always there to help us
navigate our way through life.

Video Camera

DOTING PARENTS CAN hardly wait to rush out and buy this bit of gadgetry to record the sweet, funny and monumental moments of their little darling's life. TV shows are full of these hilarious and cute videos, and clip-sharing websites thrive on contributions from amateur cameramen who happened to be there at the right time, with a lens pointing in the right direction.

Those of us who are not budding cinematographers, however, often find that when you *really* need to capture that moment, the battery isn't charged, the memory is full, or the damned thing is sitting on a shelf at home when you're miles away on a day out... Typical!

If you do remember to pack the camera when you go on holiday, or grab it when the kids are playing in the garden, you can build up a vault of precious memories. Not to mention the modern equivalent of the embarrassing baby picture – to be pulled out at home for viewing by new girlfriends and old mates when the whim takes you!

Crystal Ball

MUMS ALL HAVE A touch of the fortune-teller about them, and an uncanny knack of spotting disaster before it happens. It's part of the job description to forecast impending calamity and the spooky thing is, Mum is usually right. The evidence is clear in these familiar phrases:

- 'If you keep doing that you'll break it.'

- 'You're going to fall and break your leg.'

- 'I told you that would happen, but you wouldn't listen.'

- 'I knew you were going to say that.'

- 'It's bound to end in tears.'

When will they learn that Mum always knows best?!

Swimming Float

FOR ALL THOSE HOURS spent in the swimming pool, splashing about with baby, then teaching the toddlers to swim.

Later in life, when your kids grow up and leave home, it's sink or swim – and Mum is always the one who helps keep them afloat.

Cookies

THE SWEET, CRUNCHY taste of homecoming, a freshly baked cookie takes everyone straight back to life at their mother's knee. Cookies are the stuff of sleepless nights – when Mum lets a little insomniac sit in the kitchen with milk and biscuits – as well as being the after-school snack that never fails to boost the spirits. Whether picked up from a bakery during the walk home from school – those Frisbee-sized chocolate-chip treats that make a child's eyes as big as saucers – or baked at home together, cookies have a melt-in-the-mouth magic that simply cannot be beaten.

For young children, cookies are often among the first recipes tackled by budding chefs, who soon learn they taste a million times more magical when baked at home. With all the luxury brands on sale today, they don't have to be home-baked, but there's nothing like a bit of home cooking and they are well worth a go for a tasty teatime treat.

'Think what a better world it would be if we all, the whole world, had cookies and milk about three o'clock every afternoon and then lay down on our blankets for a nap.'

BARBARA JORDAN

White Choc Chip Cookies

An indulgent twist on the classic king of cookies.

Ingredients

>   125g (4½oz) butter
>   150g (5oz) brown sugar
>   1 egg yolk
>   1 tsp vanilla essence
>   190g (7oz) self-raising flour
>   190g (7oz) white chocolate chips or finely
>   chopped white chocolate

Method

1.   Preheat oven to 180°C (350°F, gas mark 4). Grease or line a baking tray.

2.   Place a mixing bowl over a pan of simmering water and melt the butter. Add the sugar and mix together, then remove the bowl from the pan to cool.

3.   Mix in the egg yolk and vanilla essence, then add the flour and choc chips (or chocolate) and stir well.

4.   Form the dough into balls, the size of a ping-pong ball, and place on the tray before pressing a little flatter, leaving about 4cm space between them.

5. Bake for 12 minutes on the middle shelf.

6. When done, leave for a minute or two then carefully transfer to a wire rack to cool.

'Having children made me realise how making the world a better place starts at home.'

MADONNA

Kitchen Sink

MODERN MUMS MAY not be tied to it any more but it still features heavily in family life. It's used for everything from bathing babies and washing hands before dinner to sourcing cold water for cuts, filling huge jugs with iced squash on long hot afternoons and loading water pistols for summer fun.

And it's not all about peeling potatoes and washing pans – the kitchen sink can also become your very own science lab, with fun experiments which will teach the kids a thing or two.

Vinegar Volcano

The easiest and safest scientific experiment using household products that are found in the cupboards.

You will need:

>An empty small plastic drinks bottle (500ml)
>A funnel
>1 cup baking soda
>A cup
>1 tsp washing-up liquid
>Food colouring (optional)
>1 cup vinegar

Method

1.   Place the plastic bottle in the bottom of your sink.

2.   Insert the funnel into its neck.

3.   Pour the baking soda into the bottle.

4.   In a cup, mix together the washing-up liquid and the food colouring (for a more spectacular eruption), along with the vinegar.

5.   Pour the vinegar mixture into the bottle and watch your volcano explode!

The Science Bit

Vinegar is a weak acid (acetate) which reacts with and neutralises sodium bicarbonate (baking soda). The reaction produces carbon dioxide, given off as a gas. It is the CO_2 that causes the bubbling over, or the 'eruption'.

EDIBLE CRYSTALS

This takes a few days but it's fun to set up and kids love the sweet results.

You will need:

> 3 cups sugar
>
> 1 cup water
>
> A few drops of food colouring or lemon juice for flavouring
>
> A clean glass jar
>
> A pencil
>
> String

Method

1. Mix the water and sugar in a saucepan and bring to the boil, stirring continually.

2. Allow the solution to cool for a while and add food colouring. Pour into the jar.

3. Tie the string around the pencil, leaving a strand hanging, long enough to almost touch the bottom of the jar. Place the pencil over the jar with the string hanging in the solution.

4. In three to five days crystals will magically cluster around the string. They are perfectly edible so enjoy!

The Science Bit

Water can only take a certain amount of solute (a substance being dissolved in it) before it becomes over-saturated – but when you heat it, the particles move apart and it can accommodate more. When the water cools down, it releases the excess sugar particles … which then cling to the nearest suitable surface (i.e. the string) and build on to each other to form larger crystals. Magic!

Name Labels

THESE TINY PERSONALISED squares of fabric are the enduring symbol of the first day of school. For weeks before the start of term, Mum is frantically labelling every item of clothing, every shoe and gym plimsoll, and when the big day arrives she will watch with pride as her baby puts on her name-studded uniform and becomes a pupil. A tear is wiped away as the new student, with shiny new shoes and smart school bag, takes their first steps towards the big, imposing building, constantly glancing over their shoulder to see if Mum is still there. It's a huge day in the life of both parents and child and each name label sewn in each new item is infused with emotion and love.

However, it takes no time at all for parents to discover that labelling does not always guarantee the shiny new clothes make it home. Schools are bottomless pits, capable of making endless items of property disappear without trace. An entire PE kit, labelled and embroidered with initials, can vanish into thin air, coats never get through the winter and shoes can walk off – usually one at a time.

Name Tags

Some parents saddle their kids with monikers that should never make the sew-in labels. The following, which may well raise a snigger, are – hand on heart – actual names.

1. Jed I Knight

2. Batman Bin Suparman

3. Kitty Litter

4. Pearly Gates

5. Jimmy Riddle

6. Terry Ball

7. Stan Still

8. Anna Sassin

9. Barb Dwyer

10. Paige Turner

'My mother wanted us to understand that the tragedies of your life one day have the potential to be comic stories the next.'

NORA EPHRON

Sewing Kit

THE ICY HAND OF dread grips all but the most accomplished seamstress when their primary school child announces, 'I need to dress up on Friday.' Whether it's a themed day at school or a Christmas play, the news sparks a frenzy of rummaging in drawers and dressing-up boxes, looking through the charity shop bags for clothes you can destroy and even sacrificing a favourite shirt for the greater good.

To make matters worse, there's always one mum who whips up insanely complicated costumes, producing a perfect Alice in Wonderland dress, a beautifully sewn toy soldier outfit or a shimmering king costume for the nativity at a moment's notice. The majority can only stand back and admire this model of perfect motherhood while cursing the fact that even sewing on a button remains a stretch.

For the unskilled, the sewing box is always well stocked with a myriad of coloured threads, unopened packets of needles and pristine pin cushions. But a simple act like sewing on a cub badge can produce a near nervous breakdown – especially when you've carefully stitched round it only to find you've sewn it on upside-down or, worse, stitched it to your jeans. (It happens, trust me.)

Don't panic. You don't have to be Stella McCartney to knock up an eye-catching outfit in one evening. Below are some simple designs that you can put together in a jiffy – with or without your sewing kit.

Easy Peasy Costume Ideas

Elf or Goblin

You will need:

> Red jumper or long-sleeved T-shirt
> Green jogging bottoms or leggings
> 2–3 sheets (A4) green felt
> 1 sheet (A4) red felt
> Fabric glue and/or sewing kit
> Pins or safety pins
> Black belt

Method

With the leggings and top doing most of the work for you, all that's left for Mum to rustle up are a few decorative embellishments and accessories...

1.   Take the green felt and cut 6 large equilateral triangles to go around your child's neck. The sides of the triangles should be between 7 and 11 cm, depending on the size of the child.

2.   Sew or glue the triangles around the neckline of the top, slightly overlapping each one, to create a zig-zag neckline.

3.   Now take the red felt and fold it round into a cone, to make your elf a hat. Place on your child's head to determine the correct size and pin into place. Then sew or glue the cone to hold the shape. (If using glue, flatten the material so the glue sticks firmly.) Cut excess material from the bottom to give the hat a flat base.

4.   Cut green triangles from the remainder of the green felt and glue or sew around the hat's base, pointing up the hat and overlapping to create a zig-zag effect. Wear the full oufit with the black belt to complete the look.

BUSY BEE

You will need:

        A yellow T-shirt
        5 sheets (A4) black felt
        Fabric glue or sewing kit
        Black plastic Alice band
        Black and yellow pipe cleaners

Black or yellow polystyrene balls (available from
craft shops) or table-tennis balls and acrylic
paint
Black leggings or trousers

Method

1. Cut thick strips of black felt and sew or glue
    horizontally on to your yellow T-shirt.

2. For the antennae, drill two small holes in the
    headband and thread the pipe cleaners through,
    or simply wrap the pipe cleaners round the band.

3. Push the tops of the pipe cleaners into the balls. If
    you are using ping-pong balls, paint them black
    first, then make a small hole in each one and push
    the pipe cleaner through.

4. Wear with black trousers or leggings for the full
    effect.

'I can't help but be a different person now that I've
had kids. That really does change your whole
perspective on life for the better.'

JENNIFER LOPEZ

KNIGHT CRUSADER

You will need:

      Large plain white T-shirt
      1 sheet (A4) black felt
      Fabric glue or sewing kit
      Grey hoodie
      Black tracksuit bottoms

For sword and shield:

      Cardboard (two large cereal packets or a pizza
         box will do)
      Tin foil
      Paper
      Black marker pen
      Glue
      Duct tape
      Black tape or parcel tape

Method

1.   Cut the sleeves off the T-shirt, making them short enough to just cover the shoulders.

2.   Cut out a cross from the black felt – either a straight cross or one with flared ends (known as a Latin cross). Sew or glue to the front of the T-shirt.

3.   Wear the customised T-shirt over the top of the hoodie, together with the tracksuit bottoms.

Sword and shield

If you have a young boy, the chances are you will have toy versions of these already but if not, here's a simple way of whipping up a medieval weapon:

1. Sketch a shield shape on the cardboard and cut out. Cover with tin foil.

2. Using the paper, cut out a cross design to match the one on the tunic and colour it in with a black marker. Glue on to shield.

3. Take another strip of cardboard and glue the two ends to the back of the shield, leaving a loop to hold, to form the strap.

4. On another piece of cardboard sketch the shape of a sword and cut out. (If the cardboard is very thin, double up and cut two shapes out at once, then glue them together.)

5. Cover the blade with silver duct tape (or silver foil). Then cover the handle with the black or brown tape.

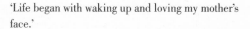

'Life began with waking up and loving my mother's face.'

GEORGE ELIOT

Mortar Board

Où est la gare sil vous plaît?

I wandered lonely as a cloud...

$24\overline{)2953.45}$

$E = mc^2$

$\mathcal{B}$ECAUSE AS SOON AS your budding professors begin to bring homework home from school, Mum is expected to be English teacher, mathematician, scientist, history buff and all-round genius. She may not be an algebra whizz, but Mum still has a few old-school tricks up her sleeve from her own pupil days. Here's a quick reminder of some of the mnemonics and memory aids that will keep Mum top of the class.

To remember the spelling of that tricky word 'because': Big Elephants Can't Always Use Small Exits.

A common but oft-forgotten way of recalling the colours of the rainbow (Red, Orange, Yellow, Green, Blue, Indigo, Violet): Richard Of York Gave Battle In Vain.

Every Good Boy Deserves Favour signifies the notes represented by the treble clef stave in music. The notes represented by the spaces between spell FACE.

'I before E, except after C' has so many exceptions, it doesn't always help. But to narrow down mistakes, there is an addition: 'I before E, except after C or when sounded as "A", as in neighbour and weigh.'

For easy calculation of the nine times table, take the number being multiplied by nine, count along your ten fingers and bend the corresponding finger down. The number of fingers to the left is the first digit of the answer, and to the right the second digit. For example, for 7 x 9 put the seventh finger down. There are six fingers to the left and three to the right, therefore the answer is 63.

Pompoms

HIGH-KICKING ROUTINES in skimpy miniskirts are *not* recommended on the school sports field – but Mum is still number-one cheerleader. Freezing on the side of a rugby/football pitch, watching endless swimming galas and running races are all part and parcel of parenthood. Avoiding the temptation to deliver an ear-bashing to the club cheat or to wade in when your lad is buried in a bone-breaking scrum is the hard part!

Packed Lunch

MUM MAKES HUNDREDS of packed lunches in a lifetime and it's good to know that the kids are getting a nutritious, filling meal even when they are away from home. Buttering bread for sandwiches late at night and rummaging round in the fridge for cheese or ham all go with the territory – as does living in a constant state of confusion over where the lids for the Tupperware boxes actually vanish to.

Keeping a packed lunch healthy and imaginative is another challenge Mum tackles on a daily basis. Cheese or ham sarnies, on white bread, are all very well on occasion but healthier options have to be considered, so here are some packed-lunch ideas to inspire you. Team them up with a little pot of grapes, a piece of fruit or a handful of cherry tomatoes – and a helping of mother's love to send kids on their way.

Tasty Packed Lunches

Nutty Banana Wraps

Ingredients

>1 banana
>
>1 tsp lemon juice
>
>1 wholemeal flour tortilla
>
>6 tbsp peanut butter, crunchy or smooth

Method

1. Thinly slice the banana and place in a bowl. Add the lemon juice to coat the banana.

2. Warm the tortilla in the microwave for a few seconds. Spread the peanut butter over the tortilla.

3.   Lay the banana slices on top of the peanut butter.

4.   Roll into a tight log and wrap in clingfilm.

NOTE: Some schools do not allow peanut products in packed lunches so best to check beforehand.

Tuna and Sweetcorn Pitta

Ingredients
>   1 wholemeal pitta bread
>   3 tbsp tuna flakes
>   1 tbsp tinned sweetcorn
>   1 tbsp mayonnaise or crème fraiche

Method

1.   Warm the pitta gently under the grill to enable opening.

2.   Cut into two and use a knife to carefully open the 'pockets'.

3.   Mix the tuna, sweetcorn and mayonnaise in a bowl.

4.   When the pitta is cool, spoon the mixture into the pocket and then wrap in clingfilm or foil. Can be refrigerated overnight.

Vegetable Pasta Salad

Serves 4

Ingredients

>225g (8oz) penne or fusilli pasta
>
>150g (5oz) cheddar cheese, grated
>
>50g (2oz) cucumber
>
>50g (2oz) cherry tomatoes
>
>1 red pepper
>
>50g (2oz) tinned sweetcorn
>
>100g (4oz) crème fraiche
>
>1 tbsp tomato ketchup

This recipe uses cucumber, tomato, pepper and sweetcorn but can be adapted to suit any favourite veg. For example, sugarsnap peas, carrots, chickpeas, beans and broccoli work well.

Method

1. Cook the pasta as directed on the packet. Drain and cool by running under cold water.

2. Place the pasta in a large bowl and add the grated cheese.

3. Dice the cucumber and half or quarter the tomatoes, then add to the bowl.

4. Chop pepper and add, along with sweetcorn, and stir.

5. Add crème fraiche and tomato ketchup and mix well.

KIDS' TOP FIVE
excuses for not eating lunch

1. I liked cheese yesterday but I don't like it today.
2. I didn't have room for the sandwich because I was saving myself for the chocolate biscuit.
3. The apple wasn't red enough.
4. I forgot.
5. I thought I'd save you the bother of making another packed lunch tomorrow.

Thermometer

THE FIRST THING Mum pulls out of the bathroom cabinet when she hears those dreaded words, 'I don't feel well', especially on a school day. If there's a temperature involved, the painful decision of whether her offspring goes to school is settled instantly. If the temperature is normal, she needs to become Sherlock Holmes to uncover the truth and deduce whether it's a genuine sickness or an attempt to swing the lead with a fake malady.

Numerous Dennis the Menace and comic book stories saw lads dipping the bulb of the thermometer in a hot cuppa to wangle a day off school, and kids are pretty crafty when a day of pampering from Mum looks set to replace a day of lessons. Thank goodness for the more modern forehead thermometers, which can give a reading in seconds. Almost fraud-proof – unless the little monster presses a hot flannel to his forehead without getting caught…

'What does good in bed mean to me? When I'm sick and I stay home from school propped up with lots of pillows watching TV and my mom brings me soup – that's good in bed.'

BROOKE SHIELDS

Chicken Soup

*F*OR CENTURIES CONCERNED mums have cooked up vats of chicken soup for their ailing children, safe in the knowledge that the warming dish will soothe, nourish and comfort. Although traditionally linked to the Jewish matriarch, every country and culture has an equivalent broth and many believe it has medicinal properties.

A study conducted at the University of Nebraska in 2000 by Dr Stephen Rennard found that some components of the soup had anti-inflammatory properties which could, hypothetically, ease cold and flu symptoms. He also surmised that the vitamins present could boost the immune system. However, in the interests of balance, he admitted the findings were inconclusive, as the study was carried out on cells in lab conditions, rather than on living human subjects, and some other soups had the same effect.

That said, he did throw the mum factor into his findings about the classic comfort food, which he termed the 'TLC factor'. He concluded: 'If you know somebody prepared soup for you by hand, that might have an effect.'

Medicinal or not, it's also a great way to use up the leftover chicken after a Sunday roast, making a cheap, tasty and nutritional meal.

'I think that women just have a primeval instinct to make soup, which they will try to foist on anybody who looks like a likely candidate.'

DYLAN MORAN

CHICKEN SOUP RECIPE

Ingredients

      55g (2oz) butter

      1 onion, peeled and sliced

      2 leeks, chopped

      2 carrots, peeled and finely diced

      25g (1oz) plain flour

      1.2 litres (2 pints) chicken stock

      450g (1lb) cooked chicken, skinned and shredded

      Salt and freshly ground black pepper

Method

1. In a large pan, fry the onions, leeks and carrots in the butter until they start to soften.

2. Stir in the flour and cook for a further minute on a medium heat.

3. Slowly stir in the chicken stock and then bring to the boil, stirring constantly.

4.   Add the chicken, season to taste and simmer for
        10 to 15 minutes, until the vegetables are tender.

Flannel

FOR MOPPING FEVERED brows, making ice packs for sprains and pains ... but mostly for scrubbing sticky faces and dirty knees. The face flannel is a weapon that has been wielded at grubby youngsters since time immemorial and has proved vastly more effective than soap and water. But mums often miss the beauty secret behind the humble facecloth. It has, in fact, natural exfoliating properties, so using on the face and body gets rid of dead skin cells without the need for expensive scrubs.

Even so, adults who swear by these squares of material for their little monsters rarely wash their own faces with them. Fifty years ago, 6 million flannels were sold annually in the UK but in recent years sales have dropped by 6 per cent, year on year. Debenhams even launched a 'Save the flannel' campaign in 2012, urging women to return to face washing as part of their beauty regime!

Urban Dictionary

NOTHING KEEPS A parent young like having teenagers in the house. As soon as they start secondary school, get mobile phones and log on to social networking sites, they begin to speak a different language altogether. After listening open-mouthed for a while, and endless entreaties of, 'Can you say that again – but in English?', Mum soon gets to grips with the modern tongue. Here are a few common phrases to help you cross the language barrier:

Pown, powned (pronounced 'pone') – dominated or won, as in owned it.
'You powned that last match.'

Hench – fit or muscular (in boys), manly (if describing a girl).
'That boy is well hench.'

Beef – argument or feud.

'Chloe and Jess won't both come because they've got beef.'

Chirpsing – flirting with (especially by text or social media sites).

'I dumped him because he was chirpsing her behind my back.'

On it – flirting with each other; almost an item but not yet official.

'Jack and Molly are on it.'

Cray – crazy.

'Friday night was just cray.'

Sick – great, fantastic.

'Have you seen this sick new band?'

Gassed – getting excited or agitated.

'I was so gassed when I got tickets for the gig.' 'Her mum was gassed because she wouldn't listen.'

Bare – very or lots.

'She's bare fit.' 'She's so rich, she has bare designer clothes.'

YOLO – 'You only live once.' As justification for a silly or crazy act.

'We're all going to the shopping mall in our onesies on Saturday. YOLO.'

A word of warning: while it's acceptable to understand your kid's teenspeak, you are NEVER permitted to use it yourself, especially if you want your teenager to talk to you again. If you want to make your offspring curl up in horror, all you have to do is say: 'Have you been chirpsing him? He's hench. I'd be well gassed if you two were on it.'

Facebook Page

IF YOU CAN'T beat them, join them! As soon as the kids reach their teenage years, social networking becomes a huge part of their lives whether we like it or not. But for mums the sites serve a dual purpose – you can keep in touch with friends, no matter how far away they are, and, more importantly, you can keep tabs on your kids. Whatever site they sign up to, make sure they accept you as a friend or follower. Not only does it allow you to keep a protective mother-bear eye on any cyber-bullying – all too rife these days – but you can also have hours of fun keeping up to speed with their all-important social lives.

Word of warning though: never forget that ALL their friends can read what you post!

TOP TEN

things to avoid on your child's social network site

1. Criticism of your son or daughter's hair/clothing/make-up/behaviour/lifestyle.

2. Bitching of any kind.

3. A telling-off – you might be furious with them but it can wait until they get home.

4. Gushy messages like 'Missing you already, can't wait 'til you come home from school'.

5. Private nicknames – if you call your darling offspring 'Snooky wooks' or 'Bunny', their friends don't need to know.

6. Family news – if Great Aunt Jane has had her corns done, their friends don't *want* to know.

7. Pictures of yourself.

8. Embarrassing pictures of your child – especially naked baby snaps.

9. Messages about their love life – they may be discussing it openly online but you chipping in with 'I think James is really fit too' is not acceptable.

10. Friend requests to your children's friends, no matter how much you like them.

> 'Children aren't happy with nothing to ignore
> And that's what parents were created for.'
>
> OGDEN NASH

Shopping Bag

A HOUSE FULL OF 'bags for life' is the legacy of all
those hours filling trolleys to put food on the family
table. Mum's world is full of handy carriers – in the boot
of the car for the unplanned stop-off on the way home from
work, on top of cupboards filled with clothes destined for
the charity shop and in kitchen drawers awaiting use as a
bin liner. Ooh, the glamour.

But it's not all about providing the family meal.
Shopping bags also mean trips to the mall for retail
therapy with pals, solo jaunts to splash out on number one,
and the joy of mother-and-daughter spending sprees.
Shopping trips with older offspring are a treat for both – as
long as they're handled right. Here are a few tips for a
happy spending and bonding experience:

- Plan in advance which shops you want to visit with
  a fair share of both your choices. You may not want
  to spend the whole day looking at the latest
  teenage trends.

● Take her fashion advice, but only up to a point. Teenage girls often have a great eye for fashion but you need to know what suits you – before she has you waltzing out in hotpants and midriff tops.

● Tell her your budget before leaving the house, and decide which items are the most necessary.

- Leave time for rest. Aching feet and heavy shopping bags mean a grumpy mum, so plan a leisurely lunch or at least a lengthy coffee break.

- Avoid underwear shopping. You might already know what's in her knicker drawer (you still do the washing after all) but she certainly doesn't want to know about your sexy lingerie.

'I've been shopping all my life and still have nothing to wear.'

ANONYMOUS

Smartphone

O MATTER HOW grown up the kids are, a mother is on call for advice, sympathy and words of wisdom 24/7. Whatever the crisis, hers will be the first number dialled and she'll drop everything to listen to the minor drama which is consuming her beloved child. And thanks to the leaps and bounds in new technology in recent years, that can be any time, anywhere.

The smartphone has revolutionised the role of a busy mum and is perhaps the closest technology has yet come to recreating her multi-tasking skills. Like her, it can organise, inform, entertain and communicate all at once; it sends reminders about birthdays and anniversaries we need to remember and gives us lists of things to do. It keeps the kids quiet with games and keeps tabs on the teenagers while they are out and about. And for the career-minded mum it means she can be in constant contact with the family while she's out at work – and even give them 'facetime' if she needs to be away. A modern marvel ... just like Mum.

Picture Perfect

In the age of camera phones and smartphones, Mum's precious 'purse photos' of her kids are now available 24/7 in all their high-tech, hi-res, full-screen glory. No longer squished between the bundles of receipts and hastily scribbled shopping lists in her big bag, the chances of innocent bystanders getting bombarded with family snaps are, admittedly, even worse. No one can escape those moments of oohing and aahing over the cute little images now that Mum has the means of carting around whole photo albums on a handy little device. She might even produce a video for good measure!

Clock

WITHOUT WHICH THE phrase 'What time do you call this?' would never pass the lips. Anyone who has ever been a teenager remembers that heart-stopping moment when you let yourself in the front door, as quietly as possible, only to find Mum sitting at the kitchen table in her dressing gown with a face like thunder. Without a doubt she has not taken her eyes off those tell-tale clock hands for hours...

The clock also keeps Mum company while she's up at all hours with her newborn – although a.m. and p.m. may cease to have much meaning.

Did You Know?

Clock and watch companies nearly always photograph their products with the time set at ten past ten. Why? Because the upright, 'upbeat' hands make it look like the clock face is smiling!

Which isn't what Mum will be doing when her teenager creeps through the front door at ten past three in the morning...

High Heels

*T*HE INSTANT GAME-CHANGER for women. The one thing, above all others, that says, 'I am woman, hear me roar!' After an hour of getting dolled up and putting on the best clobber, the skyscraper heels are the finishing touch which transforms an everyday mum into a glorious glamour-puss. They are not just a fashion item – they are a state of mind!

'I don't know who invented high heels, but all women owe him a lot.'

MARILYN MONROE

Flats

FOR THOSE 'CAN'T I go back to bed?' days and those kick-off-the-heels-after-a-hard-day's-work moments. Great for the shopping days, pushing a buggy around town and running after a wayward toddler. Best of all, they're Mum's secret weapon on school sports day. The one time you are *not* going to impress in your skyscraper stilettos. On your marks, get set...

Pair of Trainers

WE ALL HAVE good intentions when it comes to working out, but for most of us they remain just that: good intentions. It's somehow always easier to find better things to fill your time – like watching *Downton Abbey* with a nice box of chocs!

But forget expensive gyms and workout guilt – why not get active with the kids for some first-rate exercise money can't buy? From chasing after them in the garden to having a kickabout in the park, have fun and get fit as a family. Running round the garden with the kids' laughter ringing in your ears is much more fun for everyone!

Fitness Fun

Try these active ideas to get the family on their feet:

- Ball games. From football to cricket, basketball to catch, ball games will help younger kids to improve their coordination and physical skills, as well as generating great team spirit.

- Walking wonders. Explore your local countryside and turn it into an adventure on the way. Your local tourist office should be able to supply a variety of walking routes to keep things interesting.

- Garden games. Bring back old-fashioned playground fun: stick in the mud, traditional tag, running races, hopscotch and skipping.

- Dance-tastic. Put on some music and get everyone to throw some shapes. Try using different tunes – from country dancing music to pop classics – to spice things up.

'The only love that I really believe in is a mother's love for her children.'

KARL LAGERFELD

Plastic Toy

THERE COMES A time in every mother's life when she
finally gets round to clearing out her handbag, only
to find that she has been carting around a sack-load of
'free' plastic toys for several months. Each one has a story
– a shopping trip when the kids persuaded you to buy
lunch at a fast-food joint so you could get a Disney-themed
wind-up toy; a magazine that your child just *had* to read,
which was then discarded untouched in favour of the
freebie taped to the cover; the lucky dip at the village fete;
the arcade machine which blasts 'Prize every time' and
ends up dispensing a 20p gift after swallowing a quid.

These badly made 'giveaways' are the bane of a parent's
life. Obtained through pester power, your own rumbling

tummy or a higher desire to keep your kids reading, they rarely amuse the children for more than a few minutes. And when they're done cluttering up your handbag, they clutter up living rooms, toy boxes and bedrooms until you feel like you are living in a graveyard for useless and broken plastic rubbish.

It's no accident that when the writers of *The Good Life* wanted to give Tom a job that summed up the futility of the daily grind, they made him a designer of plastic toys to be given away in cereal packets!

Emergency Toy

*A*N OBJECT THAT can be *any* object. Desperate times call for desperate measures!

Picture the scenario: a crowded restaurant and a toddler who won't stop screaming, exasperated parents desperately attempting to stop the toe-curlingly embarrassing wail emanating from their table but loath to leave before their rare meal out is finished. Then horror as they realise that baby's favourite toys are all in a bag on the kitchen table at home.

That's when the over-stuffed handbag (see page 12) comes into its own. If Mum doesn't have an actual toy hidden in there somewhere, she can produce a stand-in from the usual contents of the bag. A bunch of keys is the undisputed favourite, and will keep a young child occupied for hours (mainly because he'll drop them on the floor umpteen times and delight in watching his obedient parents, grandparents etc. pick them up). But there are a few other everyday items that will prove useful in an emergency:

- A compact mirror (held by an adult or older child) can be used to throw light around the room and proves a great distraction for young children.

- A heavy necklace can be whipped off for a child to play with, under supervision (so it doesn't head straight for the mouth).

- A mobile phone. If they're old enough modern phones are like an instant entertainment centre, with games galore.

- For kids over two or three, pens and paper should be carried in your bag at all times. As well as drawing, it means they can play hangman, noughts and crosses, heads, bodies and legs and many other games.

- Any object can be 'humanised' into a new friend – a wallet that dances along the table or a key fob with a life of its own (and voice to match).

If it's winter, one of your gloves could be transformed into a simple glove puppet just by waggling your fingers; or see below for a longer-term solution.

ᑫUPPET ᑫERFECTION

You've got to hand it to Mum, she knows how to keep the kids amused when the family is out and about. A couple of simple puppets, slipped in the changing bag, is all it takes. The traditional sock monster, made from one of the many odd socks floating around, with two eyes and a mouth, has delighted generations of kids. And finger puppets can be whipped up in minutes, using an old glove that's lost its partner.

GLOVE FINGER PUPPET

You will need:

> An old glove
> Scissors
> Glue (or needle and thread)
> Shop-bought self-adhesive eyes (optional)
> Red pen or fabric for mouth
> Wool for hair
> Felt or material for 'clothing'

Method

1. Cut a finger or thumb off the glove.

2. Fold over the bottom and glue or sew to prevent fraying.

3. Stick on eyes (or small pieces of felt if not using shop-bought ones).

4. Draw mouth on with red pen or stick on a red fabric mouth, and glue strands of wool for hair.

5. Cut out required clothing and stick on to the puppet.

A CAST OF HUNDREDS

- Add a red nose, some wool whiskers, two white teeth and felt ears to make a mouse.

- Make a bird with a triangular felt bird beak and some feathers, or felt wings.

- Make a grey felt puppet and add elephant ears and trunk.

- Draw a lion's face and cut out a yellow felt mane.

- To make a pirate, add a big black hat and eye-patch and a colourful shirt.

- For a fairy, cut out a pink or purple dress then cut out some wings and stick craft gems on both. Then glue dress on the front and wings on the back and add long wool hair.

- Add long purple robes and gold crowns to make a king and queen.

Bucket and Spade

THESE SIMPLE ITEMS are eternal symbols of long summer days on the beach. Ah, those happy memories of sand in the sarnies, useless windbreaks and struggling to change into your cossie under a towel! Yet they also evoke hours of fun: paddling in the sea, catching crabs, making sandcastles, playing cricket – and laughing until the final sunbeams leave the sky.

A day on the beach is the perfect antidote to modern stresses and a great opportunity to join in activities with the kids – with not a computer game in sight. Below are a few ideas to try on your seaside break.

PICTURE COMPETITION

Get the children to separate into two or more teams (depending on how many kids you have) and send them off to collect stones, shells, seaweed and driftwood. Then they must make a picture or sculpture on the sand using the things they've found – which can then be judged (or not, if you want to keep the peace instead).

BUILD A BOAT

Dig out the inside of a rowing-boat shape in the sand and make seats. If you can find any driftwood for imaginary oars, even better. The kids can then set sail on an imaginary voyage and a wonderful adventure.

BUILD A SAND CITY

One castle is just not enough. Using the bucket and spade, stones, shells and wood, build a whole city in sand, with roads, a church, houses and – for tradition's sake – a castle with a moat.

BEACH BLOW BALL

You will need ping-pong balls and straws for each player.

Using your spade, dig a channel for each member of the family, just wide enough for a table-tennis ball to fit down, making sure they are all the same length and at least a shoulder width apart. Give each player a straw then get the player to lie down on their stomachs facing their trough. Place a ball at the end of each trough and then on 'Ready steady go' each player must blow their ball to the end of their channel. The winner is the first to the end.

To make it slightly harder, you can disqualify any player whose ball leaves the channel at any point.

Sun Cream

AS SOON AS the sun comes out, the ubiquitous cream follows. Summer just wouldn't be the same without the daily ritual of chasing the children as they scatter to the four corners of the garden to avoid being smothered with factor 40. Applying the thick white cream to the face of a small squirming child without getting it into their eyes is truly something of an art.

Naturally, you can guarantee that after 20 minutes of struggling and protesting, as soon as they are liberally doused they will jump straight in the swimming pool!

Paddling Pool

PICTURE THE SCENE – the first blazing hot day of the summer, the kids (already smothered in sun cream) waiting eagerly in their swimsuits as Mum roots through the dusty old shed for last year's pool. Half an hour later she's red-faced and out of breath from attempting to blow up the inflatable sides, only to find one of the rings has a puncture, and she's cursing the space-saving decision to buy the blow-up pool instead of its rigid-sided counterpart.

But it's all worth it in the end. The chance to splash about in the garden cranks up the fun on a hot summer day and gives Mum a chance to laze in the deckchair while the kids amuse themselves. Everyone's a winner. Plus, if it's really hot, she can cool herself down by popping her feet in the water. Careful though – the closer you are to the pool, the more the kids see you as fair game for a good soaking with a water gun!

Tent

FAMILY CAMPING HOLIDAYS are relatively cheap, lots of fun and packed full of adventure for every member of the household. Whether you pack up your own, hire a static caravan or tent, or go in for the new-fangled luxury 'glamping', camping has always been a great way to spend a vacation.

Kids will love camping in their own back garden too – set up the tent in summer and allow older kids to sleep outside for the night. It's a fantastic way to maximise summer-holiday fun without blowing the budget.

And the enjoyment doesn't have to stop in winter. Why not create a hidey-hole tent in your own front room? Drape some sheets across two chairs to fashion the perfect indoor tent for children to play in – ideal for teddy bears' picnics and the like. As the nights draw in, give the children a torch so they can play shadow puppets on the canvas walls.

Top Camping Activities

Telling Ghost Stories

While the stories need to be age-appropriate, even the youngest child loves a good fright night – as long as they can leap into Mum's arms for a safe cuddle while the tale is told.

> Think about adding sound effects to your story to up the ante – a knock on hard wood as the zombie bangs on the door, a rustle of a sleeping bag as the snake slides through the forest, and so on...

Star Gazing

Make the most of sleeping outdoors and teach your children about the night sky, pointing out the North Star, the Plough, Orion's Belt and other familiar star landmarks. There are many helpful websites these days that tell you what to look out for at different times of year and in different locations; and there are also mobile apps available that will tell you which stars you're looking at there and then.

A Campfire Singalong

You could even introduce singing in rounds or in harmonies if your children are old or ambitious enough! Good traditional songs to get the party started include 'London's Burning', 'Ging Gang Goolie', 'Hey Jude', 'Quartermaster's Stores', 'Green Grow The Rushes O', 'Alice The Camel' and – for the ideal camping weather – 'Singing In The Rain'.

Cagoule

A MAC IN A sack which proves Mum's practical side every time she produces it – like magic – from a bag at the first sign of rain.

Sadly her 'Ta-da' moments are short-lived – by the time the kids reach ten they're way too cool for a cagoule!

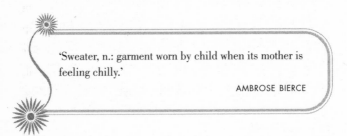

'Sweater, n.: garment worn by child when its mother is feeling chilly.'

AMBROSE BIERCE

Picnic Hamper

$\mathcal{T}$HE CLASSIC WICKER basket, complete with china plates and proper cutlery, immediately conjures up an image of long, lazy afternoons eating cucumber sandwiches on a checked blanket – with Mum dressed, no doubt, in an immaculate 1950s frock – as the children play happily in a verdant country location. These days the wicker has given way to the more practical plastic cool box, but the summer picnic has never lost its appeal. It's a wonderful – and free – way for families to meet up and socialise.

Classic sandwiches, fruit and hard-boiled eggs – served in shells and then peeled – are still the staples for a good old-fashioned picnic, but if you fancy something a little bit different, try the following cold lunch treats. (See lunch box recipes on pages 73–6 for more.)

PESTO CHICKEN WRAPS
Serves 4

Ingredients

    300g (10oz) cooked chicken
    Pesto
    4 tortilla wraps
    Handful of rocket leaves, pea shoots or iceberg
       lettuce
    Sundried tomatoes

Method

1.   Cut chicken into thin strips or shred.

2.   Spread a little pesto on each tortilla.

3.   Layer with chicken and leaves and add tomatoes to taste.

4.   Roll up tight and cut each wrap on a diagonal.

5.   Wrap each in silver foil and place in plastic
        storage box to keep shape in the picnic basket.

Feta Tabbouleh

A tasty, versatile salad which you can adapt with various
ingredients. Don't forget the forks if you are planning this
for a picnic, though. Not easy to eat with fingers!

Serves 4

Ingredients

>   30g (1oz) bulgur wheat
>   1 medium red onion, peeled
>   Large bunch fresh parsley
>   2 large tomatoes
>   100g (3½oz) feta cheese
>   3 tbsp freshly squeezed lemon juice
>   3 tbsp extra virgin olive oil

Method

1.   Put the bulgur wheat into a bowl and cover with
        50ml (2fl. oz) of boiling water then set aside for 20
        minutes.

2.   Finely chop the red onion and the parsley leaves,
        discarding stalks, and place in a serving bowl.

3.   Chop the tomatoes into quarters and discard the
        seeds, then cut into small chunks and add to the
        onion and parsley, mixing well.

4.   Dice the feta and add to the bowl, along with the cooked bulgur wheat. Stir.

5.   Add the lemon juice and olive oil and mix well.

> Optional extras: try adding cucumber, courgette, bacon, cooked chicken, peppers, beans, cooked vegetables or pine nuts to make it different every time.

VEGETABLE FRITTATA

A popular picnic dish in Italy, this is a great one for using leftover vegetables but, like the tabbouleh, can also be made with many different ingredients, e.g. ham, salami, bacon, tomato, asparagus, broccoli etc.

This is wonderful served hot with a green salad but equally lovely cold. You will need a frying pan or sauté pan which can be placed under the grill in order to prepare it.

'A mother's arms are more comforting than anyone else's.'

DIANA, PRINCESS OF WALES

Serves 4

Ingredients

      2 tbsp olive oil

      200g (7oz) diced, cooked potatoes

      1 courgette, cooked and diced

      1 red pepper, deseeded and chopped

      1 large onion, finely chopped

      5 eggs

      Handful basil leaves, roughly chopped

      Salt and pepper to taste

      80g (3oz) parmesan or gruyere cheese

Method

1.   Heat the olive oil and sauté the potatoes, courgettes, peppers and onion in a large frying pan for a few minutes, then turn the heat to low.

2.   Whisk the eggs, then add basil, seasoning and grated cheese to the bowl. Pour the mixture into the frying pan, making sure the potatoes are spread out evenly. Cook on a low heat for five minutes, until set.

3.   Place the pan under a medium grill and leave for several minutes until the top is set.

4.   Slide the frittata onto a serving plate. Leave to cool for tomorrow's picnic.

Chocolate

MUM'S SECRET LITTLE pick-me-up when the energy is flagging. She's sure to have a stash hidden from the children somewhere in the house – and woe betide anyone who so much as sniffs at it!

CHOCOLATE CHUNKS

- Chocolate was first consumed 2,500 years ago by the Mayan civilisation who – quite rightly – considered it a divine food. It was used in ceremonies and also as a form of currency. Cacao means 'god food' in Mayan.

- The record for the largest chocolate structure *ever* was an Easter egg made in Melbourne which weighed 2,033kg (4,484lb) and was 10 foot tall.

Did You Know?

The first 'Death by Chocolate' occurred in the seventeenth century in Mexico, where a church ban on the sweet stuff so infuriated the upper-class Spaniards that they poisoned the bishop who decreed it!

- Chocolate can be good for you – eating dark chocolate reduces the risk of heart disease – while it also makes you happy, raising serotonin and endorphin levels in the brain (and thereby acting as a mild anti-depressant).

- The US produces and consumes the most chocolate but, per capita, the Swiss are the biggest choc eaters followed closely by the British.

- Chocolate is craved by more than twice as many women as men.

'All you need is love. But a little chocolate now and then doesn't hurt.'

CHARLES M. SCHULZ

Duvet

TO SNUGGLE UNDER with the kids on a stormy night. To comfort them after a horrible nightmare. To throw over a poorly child when they are sick and sleepy on the sofa. For making dens, and playing pirates. And for those well-earned 'duvet days'.

Storybook

A BEDTIME STORY IS one of the most precious privileges of parenthood. It is a special time for mother and child, a chance to spend some quiet time together and settle a child down to sleep as well as to raise their awareness of books and give them a head start in literacy. Even before they can understand the words, a baby is reassured by the sound of a parent's voice as they begin to drift off.

TOP TIPS
for bedtime bliss

- It's never too early to start familiarising your baby with books. Fabric baby books and waterproof bath books are a great introduction.

- Choose bold, bright, colourful books for young babies and talk to them about the pictures. Books with different textures will stimulate their interest too.

- If it is a bedtime book, choose rhythmic, rhyming or repetitious text for babies and toddlers as the singsong nature is very reassuring, even if they don't understand all the words.

- Speak slowly and clearly, allowing them to differentiate each word, as they are picking up new ones all the time.

- Read favourite books again and again. Children love familiar tales, even if they know exactly what comes next.

- Talk them through the pictures and ask questions, e.g. Why does that farmer look cross? What is the dog carrying in its mouth?

- You needn't spend a fortune on books. Join your local library for a constant supply of new titles.

- Keep your child's favourites but arrange to swap old books with other mums so that the flow of stories keeps coming. You could even turn the book swap into a monthly girly gathering!

Classic Children's Books

For Toddlers

- *The Gruffalo* by Julia Donaldson

- *We're Going on a Bear Hunt* by Michael Rosen

- *Guess How Much I Love You* by Sam McBratney

- *Aliens Love Underpants* by Claire Freedman and Ben Cort

- *The Very Hungry Caterpillar* by Eric Carle

For 5- to 8-Year-Olds

- *Charlie and the Chocolate Factory* by Roald Dahl

- *Utterly Me, Clarice Bean* by Lauren Child

- *The Worst Witch* by Jill Murphy

- *Oh The Places You'll Go!* by Dr Seuss

- *The Tale of Peter Rabbit* by Beatrix Potter

'Stories are like fairy gold. The more you give away, the more you have.'

POLLY MCGUIRE

- *Swallows and Amazons* by Arthur Ransome

- *The Railway Children* by Edith Nesbit

- *The Hobbit* by J.R.R. Tolkien

- *The Borrowers* by Mary Norton

- *Matilda* by Roald Dahl

Mother's Day Card

BURSTING CUPBOARDS AND boxes full of toddler artwork will not deter even the most houseproud of mums from collecting these precious offerings. This one object proves, above any other, that expensive gifts are not the way to Mum's heart, and nothing is more likely to put a smile on her face – or bring tears to her eyes. The first Mother's Day card, the one sent from university and the one with a little poem scribbled inside will all have a place but it's the homemade Mother's Day card which will never see the inside of a bin – no matter how bad the drawing, or how many times a slight movement sends glitter cascading out of the drawer.

As well as an indication of how special Mum is, each card shows how important Mother's Day is. It's the one day when the tables are turned, and kids get to wait on her hand and foot. It's the day she can be pampered, spoilt and cared for and, best of all, she can find out how much she is appreciated by the whole family.

Instead of keeping all those precious bits of artwork hidden in a drawer, you could make a feature out of them. Buy a large clear picture frame, with clip fastenings, and choose a selection of your favourite home-made cards, taking care to span the ages of your children to make it more interesting. Then arrange them in the frame, as artistically as possible, overlapping each other but so the main pictures can be seen.

With one or two, you could open them so that the message inside is shown instead or – if you can bring yourself to cut them – you could separate the drawing from the message and show them both.

The ancient Greeks celebrated mothers by dedicating a day to maternal goddesses, especially Rhea, wife of Cronus and the mother of many of the Greek gods.

Early Christians honoured the Virgin Mary on the fourth Sunday of Lent. In seventeenth-century England the celebration was expanded to include all mothers and became known as Mothering Sunday.

Mothering Sunday became particularly special for servants and apprentices living away from home, who were given the day off to visit their mothers and bring gifts. This was often a fruit cake known as a simnel cake.

The custom died out in the early nineteenth century but in 1872 US activist Julia Ward Howe suggested that 2 June should become Mother's Day and be dedicated to peace, calling on all women to attend peace rallies on that day.

The modern Mother's Day in the US was founded by Anna Jarvis – who was unmarried and childless. She campaigned in honour of her own mother, a social worker, who had always wished for a day to honour mothers and their contribution to society. She and her supporters lobbied powerful people and by 1911 most states celebrated the day. In 1914, President Woodrow Wilson signed a resolution naming the second Sunday in May as Mother's Day.

In the UK, Mothering Sunday saw a revival after the Second World War, largely due to the influence of American soldiers.

Mother's Day is now celebrated in 46 countries, on different dates throughout the year.

Mothers of the World

In the Dominican Republic, families sing a special Mother's Day anthem, *Himno a las Madres*, at their gatherings. It was written in the 1920s by Trina de Moya, the wife of president Horatio Vasquez, and is taught in all schools.

In Australia, it is customary to wear a carnation on Mother's Day – a coloured bloom honours a living mother and white is worn in memory of mothers who have passed away.

Mexican sons and daughters arrive at the family home on the eve of Mother's Day and celebrate in church the following day. 'Tamales' and 'atole', the traditional early-morning meal, is taken round to all local mothers.

For those who can't decide between cake and flowers as a gift, the French have the perfect solution. Mothers are traditionally presented with a cake in the shape of a floral bouquet.

Bouquet of Flowers

*F*ROM CHEAP CARNATIONS to rare orchids to daisies plucked from the lawn, flowers are guaranteed to make Mum feel blooming special.

Autumn Leaves

*L*ONG WALKS IN the country are never more appealing than in the 'season of mists and mellow fruitfulness'. It's a great time to show children nature at its most stunning, and its most productive. As apples and pears ripen on the branches and seasonal food like corn on the cob, cobnuts and plums fill the farm shops, harvest festivals at school remind them of the bounties that nature supplies. The annual search for the prize conker is on and, with leaves turning golden brown, red and yellow all around them, children can see the seasons changing in front of their very eyes.

Autumn Activities

- Take them on a nature walk and bring a bag, or ice-cream tub, to collect fallen treasures in the woods as you stroll, e.g. conkers, bits of bark, beautiful leaves.

- Make it more interesting by showing them some of the trees and wildlife they can expect to see in the woods before leaving the house. You could even print off a picture of leaf-shapes they can tick off as they find them.

- Make a collage of the different-coloured leaves they bring home by sticking them onto paper. Or you could make seasonal greetings cards with them (see page 144).

- Take paper and crayons to make bark rubbings as you walk.

Pumpkin

WHEN THE NIGHTS draw in, Halloween is a chance for family fun: something all kids love to take part in. From toddlers to teenagers, most of them love the excuse to dress up and terrorise the neighbourhood – in the nicest possible way, of course. But when it comes to trick-or-treating, make sure the little horrors don't turn into night terrors.

TOP TIPS

for Halloween etiquette

- Keep to your local neighbourhood.

- Only knock on the doors of people you know, or who have a visible decoration outside their door or in a front window.

- Accompany younger children and, if you dress up yourself, make sure your face isn't covered and that you are recognisable.

- If older children are going alone, make sure they are in proper costumes and make a real effort – pulling a hood up and knocking on doors asking for sweets is not acceptable!

- Remember 'trick or treat' should not be taken literally – the threat of a nasty prank if householders don't cough up the goods is tantamount to demanding money with menace!

- If you are happy for local kids to knock on your door, put a pumpkin or some Halloween lights in the window.

- Keep a big bowl of fun-sized chocolate bars or packets of sweets by the front door for all the little monsters who brave your doorbell.

*H*alloween *H*ullabaloo

If you're planning a Halloween party – or if your child has a birthday around the dreaded date – here are a few ghoulish games to keep the guests entertained.

Touchy Feely Terrors

You can really let your imagination run wild on this one. Fill several small bowls with various slimy, gooey foodstuffs (tinned spagetti, hard-boiled egg, jelly etc.) and give them gruesome names (intestines, dragon's eye, ectoplasm etc.). Then get each player to come into the room, one by one, blindfolded. They must then guess what is *really* in the bowl by sticking their hand in...

Pass the Pumpkin

A spooky variation on pass the parcel. Fill a hollowed-out pumpkin with sweets and treats and bury one wrapped prize beneath the goodies. The children sit in a circle and pass the pumpkin to music, and when it stops, the child holding it picks a treat. When the last treat has gone, the next person holding the pumpkin when the music stops is the winner – and gets the main prize.

Musical Zombies

A terrifying twist on the classic musical statues game. Players must walk round in zombie style until the music stops. The first one to move in the break is out, and the music begins again. One zombie is eliminated in each round until the final player is left and declared the winner.

CARVING A PUMPKIN

1. Choose your pumpkin carefully. It should be the right shape for your design, have a flat enough surface and be relatively free of scars and blemishes.

2. Using a sharp knife, cut a large circle around the top of the pumpkin for the lid – 15 to 25 cm (6 to 10 inches) in diameter, depending on its size.

3. Cut out as much of the hard flesh as possible then scoop the rest out with a strong spoon or ice-cream scoop. Keep it in the fridge – it makes delicious soup.

4. Draw a design on the pumpkin or get the kids to do their own. For the basic Jack-o'-lantern, all you need is two eyes, a triangular nose and a jagged, toothy mouth.

5. Using a small, sharp knife, cut the design out.

6. Place a tea light candle in the base of the pumpkin to light from the inside.

Plasters

AND MORE PLASTERS! Each one with a built-in hug. If you faint at the sight of blood, parenthood is a steep learning curve. There are points in every child's life when barely a week goes by without a skinned knee or cut elbow and Mum needs to put her nurse's hat on to make it all better. Washing the wound and applying the sticky plaster may be necessary – but it's the comforting cuddle that really stops the tears.

Hot Chocolate

A CUP OF RICH, dark sweetness which radiates warmth on a cold day, a good hot chocolate is like a mother's hug – giving you a special glow inside. It's the perfect treat when the kids come in from a chilly Halloween or fireworks night, and can warm the bones after a day of building snowmen or sledging on the coldest winter days. It's the culinary equivalent of a roaring open fire – in a cup.

Heavenly Hot Chocolate

Shop-bought chocolate powders are all very well for a quick fix, but a real hot chocolate is a luxury every mother deserves. Try this simple but wickedly indulgent recipe:

Serves 4

Ingredients

> 225g (8oz) of semi-sweet chocolate (with cacao content between 50 and 75 per cent)
> 850ml (1½ pints) of whole or semi-skimmed milk
> 1 tsp vanilla extract
> 3 tsp sugar

Optional extras

> Whipped or squirty cream, for a super-indulgent topping
> A flake or grated chocolate, to crumble on the cream
> Mini marshmallows, to float on top for a sweet treat
> Rum, Tia Maria or Irish cream liqueur, for an extra kick (adults only!)

'Never mind about 1066 William the Conqueror, 1087 William the Second. Such things are not going to affect one's life ... but 1932 the Mars Bar and 1936 Maltesers and 1937 the Kit Kat – these dates are milestones in history and should be seared into the memory of every child in the country.'

ROALD DAHL

Method

1. Chop the chocolate, making sure the pieces are small enough to dissolve in the liquid.

2. Slowly heat the milk in a small pan, until it is simmering, whisking occasionally.

3. Add vanilla, sugar and chocolate and whisk vigorously. Add liqueur if required.

4. Keep on a low heat for four more minutes, stirring constantly.

5. Divide into four cups, add toppings and serve.

'Love is like swallowing hot chocolate before it has cooled off. It takes you by surprise at first, but keeps you warm for a long time.'

ANONYMOUS

Candles

A S THE SAYING almost goes, candles are not just for
birthdays. While Mum will have a store of cake
candles ready for each year's ever-more-elaborate birthday
cake creation (see page 17), there's something to be said
for the chill-out properties of the more grown-up affairs
too. Dimming the lights and relaxing on the sofa or in the
bath by candlelight can be the ideal way for Mum to enjoy
some first-class me time.

Here are five fab fragrances with their magical properties explained:

Lavender – Relaxing
The classic stress-reliever, this sweet, floral scent has calming properties which have been used to combat anxiety since the year dot. It also helps to promote sleep by relaxing the mind and body.

Grapefruit – Energising
The sharp scent of this fruit is very effective in providing an energy boost. It lifts the mood and banishes fatigue with its tangy citrus aromas.

Cinnamon – Warming
The warm, woody, spicy aroma of cinnamon is perfect for damp autumn and chilly winter days. Its comforting properties have an uplifting effect and create a cosy atmosphere. Mixed in a candle with orange or tangerine, it also produces a yummy, Christmassy smell.

Patchouli and Sandalwood – Sensual
To create a romantic atmosphere, these two are the perfect combination. The earthy, fresh fragrance of the patchouli herb is a mood enhancer and the oriental, woody overtones of the exotic sandalwood have aphrodisiac properties.

Vanilla – Soothing

The queen of aromatherapy oils, vanilla has been proven to soothe anxiety, enhance mood and lift depression. Scented candles containing vanilla are among the best at covering up any unwanted smells and its strong sweet scent is almost universally popular. It could also spice up your love life as it's a well-known aphrodisiac – especially for men!

Dressing Gown

*S*NUGGLING INTO A dressing gown on cold winter's nights gives a warm comforting feeling and Mum's dressing gown sees more action than most. Whether she's getting up to feed the baby in the middle of the night, getting up at the crack of dawn to make breakfast for older kids or to get ready for work herself, or just wrapping up after a nice hot bath, it's the snug sartorial choice for mums everywhere.

Not recommended for dropping the kids off to school though!

Posh Frock

ON THE OTHER hand, getting glammed up changes Mum into a whole new woman – whether it be for a party or a business meeting. The day-to-day household activity requires nothing more glamorous than jeans and T-shirts but everyone loves the opportunity to put on a little style. Dressing up in a smart suit for work, donning a new dress for a wedding or sizzling in a dazzling top for a girls' night out reminds a busy mother that she is still herself – and helps to unleash that inner goddess. But it pays to make sure the gorgeous new look isn't totally ruined by a dribble of baby sick on your shoulder!

TOP FIVE

fashion no-nos

1. Hotpants for the school run.

2. Double denim.

3. Flats and skinny jeans – according to Victoria Beckham it makes you look 'like a golf club'.

4. Mixed animal prints – combining leopard, zebra and snake makes you look like a walking zoo.

5. Plunging neckline with tiny mini-skirt – flash the flesh at the top or bottom, but *never* both.

Lemon

NOTHING TO DO with the sour face Mum makes when she disapproves of her child's behaviour! The lemon is a secret weapon in the day-to-day domestic world. As well as its culinary uses – including home-made cold remedies like honey and lemon, perfect for poorly kids and adults alike – the humble fruit can be used as a cleaning agent all around the home. Lemons are acidic and have antibacterial and antiseptic properties. Unlike vinegar, they make the home smell wonderful too!

ℒEMON-ᴬID

- To clean a microwave and eliminate cooking smells, put half a lemon in a non-metallic bowl, half filled with water, and zap on full power for five minutes. Then wipe the sides with a cloth.

- Mildew stains can be removed from clothes by saturating with lemon juice and rubbing in a handful of salt. Then leave to dry in the sun and wash normally in the washing machine.

- Whiten your whites by adding half a cup of lemon juice to the washing cycle and then drying in the sun.

- Put lemon juice on a clean damp cloth to wipe away soap scum in the bathroom.

- Polish brass and copper by cutting a lemon in half and adding salt before rubbing it over the metal.

- Get a shine on your windows and mirrors by mixing a litre of water with ¼ cup of vinegar and 2 tbsp of lemon juice in a spray bottle. Shake well, spray and wipe.

- Revitalise wooden furniture and floors with a mixture of one part olive oil and one part lemon juice, applied with a soft cloth.

Nail Brush

NO MATTER HOW long sports-crazy boys spend in the bath after matches, dirt always seems to linger under the nails. Only Mum's scrubbing with the dreaded nail brush will shift it and howls of protest won't deter her from her nail-scrubbing mission.

It also has plenty of uses round the house, from scrubbing the grouting between tiles to washing potatoes – although it is wise to keep different brushes for each task.

Clothes Peg

AH, THE SATISFYING pride of an outdoor clothes line strung with sparkling clean washing, flapping in the breeze on traditional clothes pegs and scented with fragrant cleanliness. A job well done!

Quite apart from Mum being the house washerwoman, those pegs could come in handy when entering a teenage boy's bedroom or changing a stinky nappy. Talk about multi-tasking...

Piggy Bank

As soon as your kids are old enough to talk, they get pretty good at asking for money. The piggy bank has been around for centuries and in many cultures it's given to infants as a good luck gift. It is certainly a great way of teaching them how to save – and the sooner that's achieved, the quicker the parental bottomless purse (see page 152) gets a respite!

Some parents have rejected the idea of pocket money and instead will give their children money when asked for, or buy them all the toys and designer clothing they want. But the age-old system of a set weekly allowance is the only way to teach them how to live within a budget, and to save for the computer games or new shoes they have set their heart on. A child who grows up without managing his own money could be in for a world of financial pain when he or she discovers credit cards and loans. And saving up for weeks for your heart's desire makes the owning of it all the sweeter.

As the children get old enough to help out, you can boost their work ethic and teach them more about personal finance by setting a fixed fee for chores. That way if they want more than their basic pocket money, they will have to use a bit of elbow grease to get it. For example, you could pay 50p for setting the table or £2 for sweeping the path. Just make sure none of the chores involve hedge-trimmers, shears or chainsaws – for obvious reasons!

Did You Know?

The origin of the piggy bank had, in fact, nothing to do with rotund farm animals. The name originated from the word 'pygg', which referred to an orange clay used to form all sorts of pottery items, including jars to hold loose change, which were named after the material itself. In the eighteenth century a clever potter decided to make a pig-shaped 'pygg bank' as a novelty item and that soon became the piggy bank of today.

Tool Kit

$\mathcal{B}$ECAUSE DAD ISN'T the only one who can turn his hand to a bit of DIY when the need arises. Mum is a dab hand at fixing household appliances and oiling rusty locks as well as altering the height of bike seats, tightening loose chains, hanging pictures etc. And it helps to have a separate tool kit – that way you can't be accused of losing his adjustable spanner next time he embarks on a 'weekend project'!

Granny

GRANNY IS THE crash mat to Mum's tightrope act. It's not just babysitting and picking up the kids from school. If she's lucky enough to still have her own mum around, she has constant back-up which goes way beyond the practical stuff. When everyone in the family is leaning on Mum, she can rely on her own mum for a bit of support of her own. When she needs to offload a bit, Granny is there to lend an ear and offer any help she can. She is always there with sage advice, practical tips and sympathetic words because, no matter how many grandchildren and great grandchildren she may have, she has never stopped being a mum herself.

The kind of parent Mum has turned out to be is hugely influenced by her own upbringing. And there comes a point in every woman's life – usually when she's shouting at the kids – when she takes a good long look at herself and says, 'Oh no, I'm turning into my mother!'

TOP TEN

tell-tale phrases that say you're morphing into Mum

1. 'I'm not made of money, you know.'

2. 'I don't care who started it, I'm going to finish it.'

3. 'Because I said so...'

4. 'What part of "no" don't you understand?'

5. 'What did your last slave die of?'

6. 'Don't you dare speak to me like that.'

7. 'You are not going out dressed like that!'

8. 'If your best friend told you to jump off a cliff, would you do it?'

9. 'When I was your age...'

10. 'Wait 'til your father gets home.'

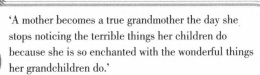

'A mother becomes a true grandmother the day she stops noticing the terrible things her children do because she is so enchanted with the wonderful things her grandchildren do.'

LOIS WYSE

'All women become like their mothers. That is their tragedy. No man does. That's his.'

OSCAR WILDE

Pancakes

WHETHER IT'S SHROVE Tuesday or a weekend breakfast treat, 'Mum's making pancakes!' prompts a scurry of little feet and raises even the tardiest teenager from their pit.

Traditionally served to use up eggs before Lent, the pancake is thought to date back to prehistoric times when roughly ground flour was mixed with milk or eggs and dropped onto a hot stone to bake. Today they provide a simple and versatile dish using the most basic of ingredients and are mainly cooked in a frying pan – which makes them a *lot* easier to toss.

A World of Pancakes

The basic pancake is served by mums all over the globe, but each nation has its own little twist on the original idea.

English pancakes are the most simple recipe, made from plain flour, milk and eggs and spread thinly around the pan. They are traditionally served with lemon and sugar.

French crêpes are closest to the English version but are usually served thinner and stuffed with savoury *or* sweet fillings. Similar crêpes are popular in Belgium, Portugal, Spain and Canada.

In the Netherlands, pancakes are thin and very large, up to 30cm (12 inches). They are served as an evening meal with a variety of toppings, resembling a pizza, as well as for dessert with sweet toppings such as fruit, chocolate sauce and ice cream. Pancake restaurants are common.

The American pancake is a small thick disc made with self-raising flour or baking powder, to make it rise in the pan, and added sugar. It is a frequent US breakfast staple served with maple syrup, blueberries or other fruits, cream, peanut butter or jam.

The Scotch pancake – sometimes called a drop scone – is closer to its American cousin than its English neighbour in size, thickness and flavour, and was traditionally cooked on a 'girdle' or griddle. They are served as a teatime treat with jam and cream, or just butter.

Scotch Pancake Recipe

Makes 6 pancakes

Ingredients

    125g (4½oz) self-raising flour
    30g (1oz) caster sugar
    Small pinch salt
    1 egg
    150ml (¼ pint) milk

Method

1.   Mix the flour, sugar and salt in a bowl.

2.   Add the egg and whisk into the dry ingredients.

3.   Add the milk, a little at a time, whisking thoroughly each time until you have a thick, smooth batter.

4.   Grease the base of a thick-based frying pan with oil then heat.

5.   Ladle in a little of the batter to make a circle of about 8 or 9 cm diameter (3 to 4 inches).

6.   After a couple of minutes, when bubbles appear on the surface, turn with a palette knife. The pancake is ready when both sides are golden brown.

7.   You may need to grease the pan again before cooking more pancakes.

Pancakes of all varieties go beautifully with maple or golden syrup, mixed berries, banana, whipped cream, chocolate sauce and ice cream, chocolate hazelnut spread, jam, honey, nuts – or as many combinations of the above as you fancy.

Paintbrush

WHEN MUM'S IN interior designer mode, there's no stopping her. She'll have those walls painted a brand new beautiful colour before you can say 'Laurence Llewelyn-Bowen'.

But it's not only about home decorating. There are plenty of arts and crafts moments when the paintbrush comes in handy. There's nothing more fun for young children than painting with Mum – and the messier the better. Whether it's potato printing, sponging or finger painting, the freedom of letting go with splashes of colour is uplifting for everyone.

Why not put the kids' creativity to good use? Try some seasonal artwork to create unique Christmas, Easter and Father's Day cards, or rustle up special and personal 'drawings' for family birthdays. You could even employ the paintbrush to create really meaningful thank-you cards (see page 173) to show your gratitude with gorgeous home-made creations.

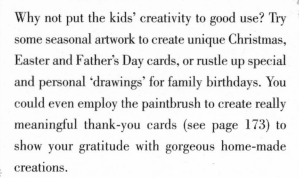

Magic Wand

Because Mum makes
everything magical.

Cushions

$\mathcal{S}$OFT AND STYLISH – just like Mum. The rest of the family may not appreciate the little touches to the household décor but cushions are an expression of taste and style, and one of the many tricks Mum has up her sleeve to make a house a home.

Every now and then, every house needs a spruce-up to refresh the look. This needn't mean splashing out on decorators or spending a fortune on a new kitchen. Here are a few cheap and easy ways to make a little difference to your home:

- Giving the walls a freshly painted look doesn't have to mean a makeover. Instead, try washing painted walls down with a solution of warm water and soda crystals. It works wonders.

- Move the furniture around to achieve a completely different perspective on things.

- Pick one plain wall in the house and make it the 'frame wall'. Cover with lots and lots of pictures in different individual frames. It can be made up entirely of family snaps, black and whites, themed photos or artwork – and the more the merrier.

If a wooden kitchen is looking a little tired, sand down and varnish the doors in a new shade. It's like a whole new kitchen for a fraction of the price. Most non-wood doors can be painted.

Add a new throw to an old sofa to brighten up a room – and of course some new cushion covers too.

Dot a room with vases of fresh flowers or house-plants for a dramatic impact.

Brighten up a boring carpet with a funky rug or two.

If you are handy with a sewing machine, you can transform a dining room by making slip covers to go over the chairs – plenty of swanky hotels and restaurants use that trick!

Cocktails

A GLAMOROUS MUM NEEDS a glamorous drink. When she's dressed up to the nines and ready to have a good time, a cocktail is just the thing to make the evening go with a swing (or a Singapore sling). Getting the party started with a Mojito or coming over all Carrie Bradshaw with a Cosmopolitan is an essential ingredient of a girls' night out.

But you don't need to be in a cocktail bar to enjoy a tantalising concoction. Slip on some sequins and a fab twenties headband and host your own flapper-style bash at home, or just invite the girls over for a raucous night in. Here are a few tipples you can mix yourself.

Classic Cosmopolitan

Ingredients

>45ml (1½fl. oz) vodka
>30ml (1fl. oz) Cointreau
>15ml (½fl. oz) fresh lime juice
>30ml (1fl. oz) cranberry juice
>Orange or lime peel for garnish

Method

1.   Chill a cocktail glass in the freezer.

2.   Shake all the ingredients in a cocktail shaker – or a clean plastic bottle with a secure lid.

3.   Strain into the cold glass.

4.   Garnish with the peel on the side of the glass and serve.

Juan Collins

Nothing to do with Joan! This is a Tom Collins with tequila instead of gin.

Ingredients

>90ml (3fl. oz) tequila
>30ml (1fl. oz) lemon juice
>1 tsp caster sugar

Ice cubes

180ml (6fl. oz) soda

Method

1.   Pour the tequila, lemon juice and sugar into a tall-sided tumbler.

2.   Add the ice and stir thoroughly.

3.   Top with soda.

WHITE WINE PUNCH

Perfect for picnics, hot summer days and barbecues. This one is to share but divide by six (approximately) for an individual tipple. This works well with almost any juice, depending on preference, although tomato is definitely not recommended! Expensive freshly squeezed varieties are not necessary.

Ingredients

1 bottle dry white wine

500ml (17fl. oz) Five Alive, cranberry or orange juice, or preferred flavour

500ml (17fl. oz) lemonade

Ice cubes

Orange slices (optional)

Method

1. Pour the drinks into a large punch bowl and mix well.

2. Add the ice and float orange slices on the top (if using).

3. Serve immediately.

Jewellery Box

*I*N THE JUMBLE OF Mum's jewellery box a host of treasures are to be found. From the elastic-and-bead bracelet made by one of the kids from a craft kit (and only worn when the immediate family is round) to the precious family heirloom which will one day pass to her own daughter or daughter-in-law, each bauble and trinket has a story to tell – and a special memory to be shared.

'Anyone may have diamonds: an heirloom is an ornament of quite a different kind.'

ELIZABETH ASTON

Make-Up Bag

*T*HIS LITTLE BAG of tricks has the power to transform Mum from, ahem, haggard insomniac to glamour queen. Gone are the dark reminders of sleepless nights, the blotches and the dreaded wrinkles, and in their place a fresh-faced beauty ready to face the world!

But that's not the only purpose of a bulging beauty bag, at least not if you have little girls. The secrets of a cosmetics collection are a source of endless wonder to these budding beauticians and hours of fun can be had as they attempt to make up like Mummy, with hilarious results. So long as it stays on their face rather than being drawn on walls and trodden into carpets, that is.

Bottomless Purse

PARENTS MAY TRY to convince their children there's a pot of gold at the end of the rainbow during the nightly bedtime story – but parents could in fact do with finding that magic booty themselves. The latest study calculated that raising a child from birth to 21 (in the UK) costs an average of £218,000. There goes the bigger house and the swimming pool!

On a day-to-day basis, there are constant calls on the wallet, from club money, lunch money and pocket money to school trips, uniform and eventually university fees. Then there are the shopping trips when the pleading gets the better of you and you end up blowing the budget on a new football or pair of shoes (for the kids, not you!), against your better judgement. If your purse is beginning to develop repetitive strain injury, think about these tips to combat pester power.

'Money is better than poverty, if only for financial reasons.'

WOODY ALLEN

- Make the distinction between 'need' and 'want', i.e. when your child says 'I really need new trainers' ask them if they mean 'I really *want* new trainers'.

- If money is tight, tell them you are only buying essentials and the 'want' items will have to come out of their pocket money. It's amazing how little they 'need' it if they have to stump up the cash themselves!

- If Christmas or birthday is looming, add those precious 'want' items to a list for relatives to choose gifts from.

- Write a list of what you intend to buy before leaving the house.

- Work out the budget and stick to it.

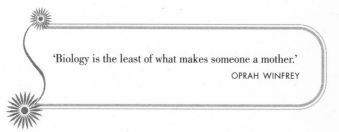

'Biology is the least of what makes someone a mother.'
OPRAH WINFREY

Scales of Justice

*I*F MUM HAS TWO or more kids, she needs the diplomacy skills of Kofi Annan and the resolve of Judge Judy to sort out disputes. And that's putting it mildly.

If even Mum's intervention fails to bring a ceasefire, and all-out sibling warfare ends with both kids storming off to their bedrooms, well, at least she gets a bit of peace and quiet... Read on to find the perfect books to indulge in while the little terrors sulk upstairs!

Paperback

FOR THOSE RARE moments of relaxation. Modern mums are so short of time that reading becomes a real luxury, reserved for the five-minute moment of peace before falling asleep, the train journey on the way to work, or those precious sun-lounger moments on holiday. Curling up with a good book, knowing she won't be disturbed before turning the page, is a very special treat indeed.

MUST-READ BOOKS FOR MUMS

When God Was a Rabbit by Sarah Winmam
A funny and moving story of an eccentric family, the love between a brother and sister, and a long-lost friendship.

The Secret Life of Bees by Sue Monk Kidd
Set in the American South in the 1960s, this is a charming coming-of-age story about 14-year-old Lily, who longs to find out more about her mother.

In the Company of the Courtesan by Sarah Dunant
Nothing to do with motherhood but a cracking read. Set in Renaissance Italy, Fiammetta and her dwarf companion, Bucino, head for a new life in Venice.

The Liars' Club by Mary Karr
A memoir covering the author's chaotic childhood in Texas, with an alcoholic father, a sassy sister and a much-married mother whose secrets threaten to destroy the family.

I Don't Know How She Does It by Allison Pearson
A sharply observed, hilarious novel about a mother trying to 'have it all'.

How to Be a Woman by Caitlin Moran
Described by *Grazia* magazine as 'the book every woman should read', this part-memoir, part-call-to-arms is a warm, funny, intelligent take on modern feminism and modern female life.

The Help by Kathryn Stockett

Now an Oscar-winning film, the story centres on an aspiring author in the era of the American civil rights movement, who decides to write about the daily struggle of the black population through interviews with a domestic servant. An informative *and* uplifting read.

Face Pack

ANOTHER WAY FOR Mum to relax, as well as being part of the beauty routine that keeps her looking gorgeous and leaves her skin soft and silky for cuddles. Scaring the pants off the kids, as she emerges from the bathroom like the creature from the Black Lagoon, is all part of the fun.

Home-Made Face Packs

Yummy Yoghurt Pack

The yoghurt has an astringent and softening effect while the oatmeal exfoliates and honey helps to retain moisture.

Ingredients

> 1 tbsp oatmeal, finely ground
> 1 tbsp plain live yogurt
> 1 tsp honey

Method

Mix the oatmeal and yoghurt in a bowl. Warm a spoon in hot water then use that to add the honey to the mixture and stir well. Apply and leave for ten minutes. Rinse off with warm water and a flannel and moisturise.

It's No Yolk

For moisturising and softening.

Ingredients

> 2 egg whites
> 2 tbsp plain yoghurt

Method

Mix the ingredients in a bowl and apply. Leave for five minutes then rinse face with warm water and flannel.

Avocado Face Food

Avocado has natural moisturising qualities and helps to renew skin cells. This treatment is good for dry skin.

Ingredients

 1 avocado (very ripe)
 1 tsp honey

Method

Mash the avocado until it is creamy and smooth then mix in the honey. Apply and leave for ten minutes then wash off with warm water.

'Having a child is a real eye-opener. It also gives you a new sense of beauty, because you feel more centred.'

CHRISTINA AGUILERA

Toothbrush

Because the glow from a mother's smile
can light up a room.

Apron

Because there's nothing like
Mum's home cooking.

Store Cupboard

AN EMPTY FRIDGE and nothing in the freezer might faze some, but mums are miracle-workers when it comes to whipping up a meal from nothing. The store cupboard is not just the place she rummages frantically through for donations when the harvest festival service comes around again. It is her secret weapon. Among those jars, packets and tins is a tasty meal just waiting to happen.

Store Cupboard Meals

You come home from a busy day at work and you haven't had time to go shopping. Do not despair. Have a good look in the cupboard and try the following easy recipes:

TUNA PASTA
Serves 4

Ingredients

> 450g (1lb) pasta shapes, such as penne or fusilli
> 3 tbsp olive oil
> Half an onion, diced (optional)
> 1 tin tomatoes, diced
> 2 tins tuna fish
> 1 tbsp dried basil

Method

1.   Cook the pasta according to instructions.

2.   Heat the olive oil in a large pan and fry the onion for a few minutes until soft. Add the tinned tomatoes and simmer for five minutes to reduce. Stir in the tuna flakes and herbs.

3.   Drain the pasta, stir into the sauce and serve.

LENTIL LASAGNE
Serves 4

Ingredients

200g (7oz) red lentils
1 large onion, chopped
1 garlic clove (optional)
1 tbsp olive oil
1 vegetable stock cube
1 tin chopped tomatoes
1 tbsp tomato puree
1 tsp mixed herbs
570ml (1 pint) milk
50g (2oz) cornflour
200g (7oz) cheddar cheese, grated
225g (8oz) lasagne sheets

Method

1. Place the red lentils in a pan and cover with water, then boil for 15 minutes.

2. Fry the onions (and garlic if using) in a little olive oil then add to the lentils.

3. Add the stock cube and stir in the tinned tomatoes, tomato puree and herbs and turn to a very low heat.

4. Now make the cheese sauce. Combine a little of the cold milk with the cornflour in a pan to make a wet paste. Then add a little more milk and stir thoroughly with a wooden spoon.

5. Place the pan on the hob, adding milk gradually and stirring constantly. A sauce whisk can help if lumps start to form. Bring to the boil, stirring constantly, then remove from the heat. Add most of the cheese, leaving enough to top the lasagne.

6. In a large lasagne dish, layer the lentil mix and lasagne sheets, ending with a layer of lasagne.

7. Top with the white sauce and sprinkle the remaining cheese on top.

8. Bake in the oven at 200°C (400°F, gas mark 6) for 30 minutes, or until the top is golden brown.

Lullaby

No MATTER HOW awful the singing voice, Mum's natural instinct is to sing to her baby – when no one's listening, of course (don't forget about that baby monitor!). Your child loves the soothing sound of your singing voice as they are lulled off to sleep.

There's no better way to wish your child sweet dreams and sweet sleep than to croon to them as their heavy eyelids start to droop and they drift off peacefully into a snug and simple slumber. Here are five top tunes to make your melodies magical:

'Twinkle, Twinkle, Little Star'
This classic nursery rhyme is based on an 1806 English poem called 'The Star' by Jane Taylor, while the tune comes from the French song 'Ah! Vous dirai-je, Maman', which dates back to 1761. While only the first verse is widely known, there are actually five stanzas to the poem. Plenty to learn if baby's slow to slumber...

'Rock-a-Bye Baby'
A ditty of confusing origins straddling the Atlantic, this tune was first published in print in *Mother Goose's Melody* circa 1765.

'Hush Little Baby'

This simple song all about the gift of a mockingbird (and more) entreats children to be quiet by shamelessly bribing them with assorted worldly gifts.

'You Are My Sunshine'

A popular number from the 1940s, written by Jimmie Davis and Charles Mitchell, which sums up exactly how your snoozing baby centres your world.

'Lavender Blue'

This seventeenth-century English folk song was nominated for an Academy Award for Best Original Song in 1949 – suitably star-studded success for your little one to dream their dreams to.

Did You Know?

Many mums start singing to their babies while they're in the womb, but recent research shows that the best music for the unborn child is rock or pop with a heavy beat. While music and voices are muffled, the baby can hear the beats and will then recognise the song they have heard when they are born.

Christmas Tree

CHRISTMAS COMES BUT once a year and for mums that's quite often enough. The most exciting time of the year for kids is made possible, and fun, by months of frantic activity behind their backs, buying and wrapping presents, preparing the house for the onslaught of family and buying and cooking the mountains of food needed to feed them all.

The Christmas tree is the centrepiece of the celebrations – the heart of Christmas around which everyone gathers to exchange gifts and embraces and thanks. With the lights sparkling in the dark afternoons, the shiny baubles reflecting children's happy smiles, it's a memory that will stay with Mum forever.

On the actual day, Mum is more of a swan than a Christmas turkey – looking serene and calm while furiously paddling away below the surface. It's not until the last mouthful of Christmas pud is served that she can finally relax. But Christmas is magical for Mum too, especially when the children are young. The glowing faces and squeals of joy are all the thanks she needs for all that hard work. The odd present doesn't go amiss though!

'Christmas waves a magic wand over this world, and behold, everything is softer and more beautiful.'

NORMAN VINCENT PEALE

Best Ever Christmas Pud

Shop-bought Christmas puddings are so much better than they used to be but nothing beats a home-made one. As it's best made months in advance, it has the added bonus of being out of the way long before the list of seasonal chores starts growing. Don't forget to get everyone in the family to stir the mixture three times and make a wish!

You will need a two pint pudding bowl for this recipe.

Ingredients

      60g (2oz) self-raising flour

      2 tsps mixed spice

      110g (4oz) breadcrumbs

      110g (4oz) suet (a vegetable variety is available
        for vegetarians)

      80g (3oz) Demerara sugar

      60g (2oz) glacé cherries

      350g (12oz) mixed dried fruit

      30g (1oz) mixed peel

      1 orange

      1 lemon

      1 apple

      3 eggs

      80ml (3fl. oz) brandy or port

Method

1. Sift the flour into a mixing bowl and add the mixed spice, breadcrumbs, suet and sugar. Mix well.

2. Quarter the cherries and add into the bowl with the mixed fruit and peel and stir.

3. Grate rind from the orange and lemon into the mix then juice both and add.

4.   Core and grate the apple into the bowl.

5.   Beat the eggs and add to the mix, stirring well.

6.   Add brandy or port – stir three times and wish.

7.   Grease the pudding bowl and add the mixture, packing it down. Then cover bowl with foil and tie round the top with string.

8.   Place an old saucer on the bottom of a large pan and fill with water, so that it comes below the lip of the pudding bowl.

9.   Boil the pudding for at least eight hours. Make sure the water is constantly topped up – if it boils away the bowl will crack and your Christmas will be ruined.

        You can boil for a few hours on different days. The pudding can't be over-boiled, but should never be under-boiled, so more than eight hours is fine.

10.   On Christmas day, boil one last time for about an hour, while the family are tucking into the turkey.

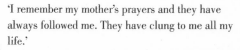

'I remember my mother's prayers and they have always followed me. They have clung to me all my life.'

ABRAHAM LINCOLN

Christmas Stocking

OF COURSE, EVERYBODY knows it's Father Christmas who *actually* stuffs the stockings for the kids, but it's still the highlight of the seasonal preparations for Mum – she gets to be Santa's Little Helper for the evening.

Preparing for the big man's arrival brings the fun of Christmas home to adults like nothing else. First there are the letters to Santa, complete with squiggly handwriting and spelling mistakes that the Enigma code-breakers would have trouble deciphering. Then it's Christmas Eve and the children's faces beam with delight as they hang their stockings at the fireplace, or from the end of the bed. Next comes the final touch, when the kids are all warm and cosy in their pyjamas and you put out the glass of port and a mince pie for Santa – not forgetting the carrots for the reindeer.

Christmas morning wouldn't be the same without the shouts of glee as the kids dive into their haul, Mum and Dad still half-asleep in their dressing gowns and getting ready to 'ooh' and 'aah' over every item that emerges. The contents of the carefully stuffed stockings (which are now more like sacks than the woollen sock of old) are soon scattered about the room as the kids ignore the traditional orange and go straight for the chocolate – before the thought of breakfast has even entered their heads.

There are many myths and legends surrounding the true origin of the Christmas stocking, but the most popular story, which goes all the way back to St Nicholas himself, also explains the fresh orange which is traditionally placed in the toe.

Nicholas was a fourth-century bishop in the city of Myra, in modern-day Turkey. In the city lived a nobleman who had squandered his wealth in the wake of his wife's death. Penniless, he was unable to provide a dowry for his three daughters, meaning they could not be married. On hearing of their plight, St Nick – as he was to become – dropped three bags of gold down the chimney, one for each daughter, which fell into the recently washed stockings that had been hung by the fireplace to dry.

The story led to the custom of hanging out stockings for Father Christmas, or St Nicholas, to fill; and the bags of gold evolved into balls of gold, represented by the orange.

Batteries

NO EXPERIENCED MUM ever greets birthdays or Christmas unless she's armed with a huge selection of these little necessities. That all-singing, all-dancing toy may send a child into delighted raptures but if it features the words 'Batteries not included', parents need to have a stockpile on hand at all times. It's not uncommon to find mass-market toys which are cheaper than the cost of the batteries to go in them, so well-intentioned gift-givers should take note. Stick to a board game or old-fashioned wooden toy – or you may find yourself off the Christmas card list!

'I once bought my kids a set of batteries for Christmas with a note on it saying, "Toys not included."'

BERNARD MANNING

Screwdriver

THE PARTNER IN crime for the aforementioned batteries. A screwdriver may be handy for whipping up the odd bookshelf and putting together the flat-pack furniture – but the main reason Mum can't live without a screwdriver in a houseful of kids is to mastermind the constant changing of batteries.

The modern world may have brought progress in many areas, but when it comes to toys, electronics have proved a backward step as far as parents' patience and pockets are concerned. Robot toys and crying baby dolls eat batteries for breakfast and anything with a remote control is double trouble, with constant replacements needed in both the toy and its master. And every single time, there's that tiny screw with the burred edges that is almost impossible to remove.

To make matters worse, every toy they receive for Christmas and birthdays is *screwed* into the packaging. What is that about?! The only purpose it serves is to add to parental stress as they battle to release a Barbie doll from the 25 screws holding her in place, with an excited little face beseeching you to *go faster!* all the time.

The Thank-You Note

THE THANK-YOU NOTE is a recurring feature in a mother's life. A new baby brings with it a host of generous offerings from friends and family, all of which need to be properly acknowledged by Mum herself, while as the kids grow older, nagging them to send their own messages of thanks is second nature in the wake of Christmas and birthdays.

In this age of internet and email, the handwritten thank-you note is worth its weight in gold – both from Mum and kids alike. Relatives will ooh and ahh as kids' handwriting improves over the years, while those oversized kisses and misshapen hearts that children sign off with say thank you in the warmest possible way.

Photo-based thank-you cards are all the rage these days. Buy a pack of plain cards from a stationers, print out a recent picture of your child – possibly enjoying the gift you're saying thank you for – and stick the image on the front. You can buy decorative wording in silver and gold for a bit of sparkle, or why not decorate it yourself for a really personal touch?

Family Noticeboard

ALONG WITH THE chock-full family calendar, the kitchen noticeboard holds the secret to keeping the family wheels well oiled. Here you will find the reams of letters that come with the average child – the details of the school trip, the packing list for cub camp, the form to be filled in for a music class, the invitation to a birthday party and so on. Here Mum has pinned all the communiqués that really matter, while deftly dispensing of those which can be ignored. And constant pruning is required. A drawing pin can only hold so much before the whole lot ends up on the kitchen floor...

'I balance work with motherhood with great precision. I plan everything in advance... We have charts, maps and lists on the fridge, all over the house. I sometimes feel like I'm with the CIA.'

KATE WINSLET

Secretary Specs

WHETHER MUM GOES to work or not, she needs to be up on her admin skills to keep the home ticking over in her spare time. Modern life comes with a lot of paperwork, online research and generally 'sorting things out'. As well as juggling the letters and forms from schools, there are all kinds of insurance to buy, bills to pay and finances to arrange. Supermum really needs to call on all her powers – especially when it comes to making phone calls to companies who are hell-bent on keeping you on hold...

Tips for Keeping on Top

1. Keep a 'to do' list on your computer or phone, and remember to look at it regularly.

2. Keep post which needs to be dealt with separate from the items that just need to be filed. Have a letterbox or rack in a prominent place so you see it often.

3. Keep e-mails that need to be dealt with in a separate folder in your inbox and check it regularly.

4. If you have a tendency to put things off, set aside half an hour a week to start your admin. Make sure you won't be disturbed and set an alarm to tell you when the half an hour is up. If the correspondence isn't dealt with in that time, set another half an hour later in the day, or the following day.

5.   If something needs to be done by a certain date, such as making a payment, set a reminder on your phone the day before, so you don't miss the deadline.

6.   Remember the feeling of satisfaction you get when something you've been putting off dealing with is finally sorted!

Snowman

THAT FIRST FLURRY of winter snow sends the kids into a frenzy and opening the curtains in the morning to a world of pure white never loses its magic. They can't wait to get their wellies on and trek out into the smooth, unbroken stillness, getting stuck into all the fun that snow brings – snowball fights, sledging, snow angels, igloo building and so on.

The snowman is the proud embodiment of all that winter fun, standing tall until the last icicle has melted and the grass is poking through the sludge.

'The first fall of snow is a magical event. You go to bed in one kind of a world and wake up in another quite different, and if this is not enchantment then where is it to be found?'

J. B. PRIESTLEY

🦋 THE PERFECT SNOWMAN 🦋

1. For the base, start with a large snowball and roll it around to allow it to pick up more snow until it is large enough. This method is quicker and packs the snow tighter than building from the bottom up.

2. Repeat to make a medium-sized ball and a small ball for the torso and head. If you want a more solid snowman, make the first ball bigger and miss out the torso to create a short chubby chappy.

3. To build the figure, pile snow on the base ball first, then place the second ball on top. Push plenty of snow around the balls where they join, packing it tightly to make sure they don't roll off at the first sign of a thaw.

4. Dress with old hats and scarves, use twigs or seaside spades for arms, and bring buttons, stones, clothespegs and the traditional carrot into play for the face.

Why not make a whole snow family and give them all names? Add a dog or cat too if you're feeling adventurous.

The Instant Snack

LIKE BABY BIRDS, the human child comes with the constant cry of, 'Mum, I'm hungry!' A stream of healthy nutritious snacks pours out of the kitchen and Mum is on call at all times to make and dispense them. Over the years, she becomes an expert at whipping up a tasty treat to satisfy these hungry little mouths and stocking up the fridge with the right foods to stop them raiding the sweet cupboards or stuffing their faces with crisps.

Here are some quick, healthy ideas for their next snack attack.

CHOCOLATE DIPPED STRAWBERRIES

Melt some dark chocolate in a bowl, over a pan of boiling water. Allow to cool slightly then place on a table with a bowl of strawberries, and get the kids to dip in and enjoy. A great way to encourage fruit-shy kids to get one of their five a day.

CHEESE AND APPLE CHUNKS

Take half an apple, 30g (1oz) of cheddar or Swiss cheese, and 30g (1oz) smoked ham or turkey. Chop into cubes and mix in a bowl.

FRESH BERRY SMOOTHIE

Ingredients

      225ml (8fl. oz) semi-skimmed milk

      1 banana

      4 strawberries

      1 tbsp vanilla-flavoured yoghurt (or plain
         yoghurt and 1 tsp vanilla essence)

      1 tsp honey

Method

Put all the ingredients in a blender and blend until smooth.

INSTANT CHEESECAKE

Spread a digestive biscuit with cream cheese and then add
a little jam. Yum!

CHEESE AND PICKLE FINGERS

A slight twist on the ultimate British comfort food, cheese
on toast.

Ingredients

>   2 slices of wholemeal or granary bread
>   100g (4oz) cheddar cheese
>   2 tbsp pickle or chutney

Method

1. Lightly toast the bread then spread a tablespoon of
    pickle on each one.

2. Grate or thinly slice the cheese and spread evenly
    on top of the pickle, making sure you get to the
    edge of the toast.

3. Pop under the grill until the cheese is browning
    and bubbling.

4. Allow to cool for a few seconds then slice into
    fingers.

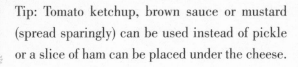

Tip: Tomato ketchup, brown sauce or mustard (spread sparingly) can be used instead of pickle or a slice of ham can be placed under the cheese.

Egg Cup

SOFT-BOILED EGGS LOVINGLY served with toasted soldiers are a staple food of childhood. Long into adulthood the act of cutting a slice of toast into strips and dipping into the creamy yellow yolk brings a flood of nostalgia and eating it with a spoon is never quite the same.

Eggs are the perfect fast food. They are cheap, quick to cook and versatile, and are naturally rich in essential nutrients including vitamin B2, vitamin B12, vitamin D, selenium and iodine.

NOTE: Official advice in the recent past has suggested that soft-boiled eggs, or any egg with runny yolks, should not be given to children under six. But attitudes are now changing, due to extensive vaccination programmes against salmonella, and eggs that are stamped with the official 'Lion Mark' are unlikely to be unsafe.

Egg Mug

This isn't just a big egg cup – but a tasty variation on the traditional 'dippy egg and soldiers' which my mum used to give me whenever I was feeling poorly. My kids love it too.

One small portion is usually enough for a child, but for older children and adults you may want to double the quantity.

Ingredients

1 large egg
1 slice of bread and butter
A mug

Method

1. Put the egg into a pan of cold water, so that it is covered.

2. Bring the water to the boil, then remove from the heat and leave in the hot water for three minutes exactly.

3. While waiting for the egg to cook, cut the bread and butter into small squares (about 1cm) and place into the mug.

4. When the egg is cooked, remove from the hot water and run briefly under cold water.

5. Using an egg cup or tea towel to hold the egg, crack off the top and spoon the entire contents into the mug on top of the bread.

6. Mix the egg and bread well and serve with a spoon.

Chick Flick

*T*HE PERFECT NIGHT in is a bunch of friends, a big bowl of popcorn and a great girly movie. Whether it's funny, feelgood or slushy and romantic, it's the one Mum's been saving up for the girls because it's wasted on the man in her life. The only mystery is why she loves to watch a movie that is guaranteed to leave her in tears...

SOFA SO GOOD
TEN PERFECT CHICK FLICKS

THE NOTEBOOK

An old man in a retirement home (James Garner) reads a moving love story to a fellow resident (Gena Rowlands) from a notebook. Flashbacks tell a Romeo and Juliet tale set in the 1940s starring Rachel McAdams as a rich Southern heiress who falls for a poor country boy, played by Ryan Gosling. After her parents forbid her to see him, and move away, war breaks out and she meets another man.

Weepy factor: 10.

MAMMA MIA!

The best feelgood movie of the past decade. Amanda Seyfried is about to tie the knot on the Greek island home of her mother (Meryl Streep) but before she does she is determined to find out which of her mum's four former lovers is her father, so he can walk her down the aisle. She invites all four to the wedding, to the horror of her mum. Meryl, Pierce Brosnan, Colin Firth and lashings of Abba. What's not to love?

Feelgood factor: off the scale.

BRIDESMAIDS

The female answer to *The Hangover* sees Kristen Wiig as Annie, whose life is spiralling downhill when her one constant comfort, her best friend Lillian, announces her engagement. Determined to be the perfect maid of honour, she finds herself in competition for the best friend title from a beautiful and stylish newcomer, played by Rose Byrne.

Laughter factor: giggles galore.

SEX AND THE CITY

Shoes, shopping and girly chats get the big-screen treatment as heroine Carrie Bradshaw prepares to walk down the aisle with her Mr Big. But one of her three best friends – played by Cynthia Nixon, Kristin Davis and Kim Cattrall – unexpectedly puts a spanner in the works.

Fabulous factor: sky high.

27 DRESSES

More wedding fun starring Katherine Heigl as a single girl who has walked down the aisle 27 times – as a bridesmaid. When her little sister (Malin Akerman) bags the man she's been secretly in love with for years, she faces the toughest wedding stint of all. Comic capers perfect for a girls' night in.

> Glamour factor: dresses to impress.

BRIDGET JONES'S DIARY

Renée Zellweger is the classic chaotic singleton torn between handsome cad Daniel (Hugh Grant) and her Mr Darcy, played by Colin Firth. The first film is by far the best so make sure you start at the beginning.

> As Bridget might say: Men fighting over wanton sex goddess, 2; snogs, 7; laughs – loads.

THE DEVIL WEARS PRADA

Anne Hathaway attempts to forge a career in fashion magazines by starting at the bottom, as a put-upon secretary to haute couture harridan Meryl Streep, editor of *Runway* magazine. High fashion and high jinks make a perfect ensemble.

> Fashion factor: catwalk queen.

CLUELESS

Alicia Silverstone stars in a modern and hilarious take on Jane Austen's *Emma*, as an LA teenager acting as match-maker to her high-school pals while twisting her adoring dad round her little finger. Stands up to the test of time after nearly 20 years – and a great one to watch with teenagers.

Sass factor: works it *and* owns it.

EAT PRAY LOVE

Julia Roberts is a recent divorcee who goes on a long trip around the world to rediscover herself through the food of Italy, the spiritualism of India and the romance of Bali.

Spiritual factor: simply special.

MOULIN ROUGE

A beautiful, sumptuous and addictive musical set in Paris in 1899. Nicole Kidman is a celebrated courtesan coveted by a jealous duke, and Ewan McGregor is a poverty-stricken poet who falls passionately in love with her. The stunning period costume and sets couple with the twentieth-century songs to show-stopping effect.

X factor: oh yes.

'When your mother asks, "Do you want a piece of advice?" it is a mere formality. It doesn't matter if you answer yes or no. You're going to get it anyway.'

ERMA BOMBECK

Perfume Bottle

*F*ROM THE MOMENT a baby is born, it has a highly developed sense of smell and for the first few months he or she prefers the scent of their mother to any other. Her unique fragrance is instantly soothing – even if she hasn't had time to shower for a week.

Growing up, little girls are also fascinated with their mums' perfume bottles – particularly the old-fashioned type with the puffer. And there can't be many mums who have escaped the thoughtful gift of the home-made perfume – a sludge-coloured liquid made from crushed rose petals and water. Delightful.

Globe

IN THE BEGINNING, Mum is the centre of every child's
world. But it's also her responsibility to show them
what a wide, wide world is out there, and to open their
eyes to what lies beyond her apron strings.

Sweet Sayings From Around the World

- *China*: To understand your parents' love you must
  raise children yourself.

- *Germany*: Parents should give their children two
  things: roots and wings.

- *India:* God couldn't be everywhere, so he gave each family a mother.

- *Switzerland:* Mum is the best – and if Mum isn't happy, nobody is happy.

- *Sweden:* Small children, small problems; big children, big problems.

- *Africa:* What the child says, he has heard at home.

- *Denmark:* Who takes the child by the hand, takes the mother by the heart.

- *China:* There is only one pretty child in the world, and every mother has it.

- *Spain and Mexico:* You only have one mother.

'To a child's ear, "mother" is magic in any language.'
ARLENE BENEDICT

Superwoman Cape

Because all mums ... are superheroes.